MW00484713

"Every Christian should thi[nk about] God. Jesus is the victor, the Savior, the deliverer, the light, the life, the way and the bread and water of life that we all need. His presence in our lives ensures that we will have access to everything. Many stumble trying to gain the blessings of God without His presence. John Belt has provided believers with a guide that is simple, practical and insightful to help us all. *The Secret to Experiencing God's Presence* will provide you with a heartfelt, panoramic view of Christian living. Study this book and learn to walk in the reality of God's presence every day!"

Joan Hunter, author and evangelist, joanhunter.org

"Some teach or write like an armchair coach having never entered the game, or others display their principles only as a theorist. John Belt writes as a practitioner! This man lives his message. I know firsthand the growth, increase and stature of this man and his ministry. John worked full-time with me for five years, and we have remained in relationship since. As a father in the faith, I am delighted to see John emerge from the inner court long enough to share with you secrets of how you, too, can live a life filled with the presence of God."

James W. Goll, God Encounters Ministries,
life language trainer, bestselling author

"Growing in intimacy with God is a foundational commitment of mine and has been since the moment I encountered His manifest presence. With biblical clarity and personal testimonies, John Belt reveals the building blocks of lifestyle intimacy. I believe *The Secret to Experiencing God's Presence* is a powerful resource full of transformative revelation and practical applications for your journey to deeper connection with God."

Dr. Ché Ahn, president and founder, Harvest International Ministry; founder, HRock Church, Pasadena, California; international chancellor, Wagner University

"John Belt has written a great book on experiencing God's presence. This book is refreshing, heart-drawing and life-giving. It reminds me, convicts me and encourages me to put first things first. Why? So that I may prosper and succeed in every aspect of my walk with God. Thanks, John!"

Barbara J. Yoder, lead apostle,
Shekinah Regional Apostolic Center

"Secrets are meant to be discovered by those hungry for life-changing insight. John Belt masterfully guides you to discovery in *The Secret to Experiencing God's Presence*. It is a unique blend of uncovering the deepest mysteries interwoven with the most practical application. His path is biblical, his book profound and his prophetic insight transforming."

Dr. Clarice Fluitt, founder and president,
Clarice Fluitt Ministries

"If you want to find your own Promised Land with God, find a pioneer who is leading the way and follow. And to make sure you are following the right pioneer, choose one who has lots of stories to tell of past pioneering successes and failures. Learn from his or her mistakes and emulate much of what you learn along the way. One such pioneer is John Belt! Many books can be written about obeying God, but precious few are written about living in His presence in your daily experiences. That is because *presence living* can only be taught by those who are actually living it. Get this book! It changes everything!"

Steve Shultz, founder and president, The Elijah List

The
SECRET
to Experiencing
GOD'S
PRESENCE

The
SECRET
to Experiencing
GOD'S
PRESENCE

JOHN BELT

Chosen

a division of Baker Publishing Group
Minneapolis, Minnesota

© 2018 by John Belt

Published by Chosen Books
11400 Hampshire Avenue South
Bloomington, Minnesota 55438
www.chosenbooks.com

Chosen Books is a division of
Baker Publishing Group, Grand Rapids, Michigan

Printed in the United States of America

All rights reserved. No part of this publication may be reproduced, stored in a retrieval system, or transmitted in any form or by any means—for example, electronic, photocopy, recording—without the prior written permission of the publisher. The only exception is brief quotations in printed reviews.

ISBN 978-0-8007-9878-9

Library of Congress Cataloging-in-Publication Control Number: 2017963663

The information in this book should not be construed as prescribed health-care advice or instruction and is not intended to take the place of consultation with health-care professionals. The author and publisher disclaim all responsibility for any liability, loss, or risk, personal or otherwise, which is incurred as a consequence, directly or indirectly, of the use of and/or application of any of the contents of this book.

Unless otherwise indicated, Scripture quotations are from the New King James Version®. Copyright © 1982 by Thomas Nelson, Inc. Used by permission. All rights reserved.

Scripture quotations identified AMPC are from the Amplified® Bible, copyright © 1954, 1958, 1962, 1964, 1965, 1987 by The Lockman Foundation. Used by permission. (www.Lockman.org)

Scripture quotations identified ESV are from The Holy Bible, English Standard Version® (ESV®), copyright © 2001 by Crossway, a publishing ministry of Good News Publishers. Used by permission. All rights reserved. ESV Text Edition: 2011

Scripture quotations identified NASB are from the New American Standard Bible®, copyright © 1960, 1962, 1963, 1968, 1971, 1972, 1973, 1975, 1977, 1995 by The Lockman Foundation. Used by permission. (www.Lockman.org)

Scripture quotations identified KJV are from the King James Version of the Bible.

Cover design by Brian Bobel

18   19   20   21   22   23   24   7   6   5   4   3   2   1

To my wonderful wife,
Brandi,
and my awesome, amazing boys,
Nethaniel and Malachi

Contents

Foreword by Patricia King   11

Acknowledgments   15

Introduction: *The Essential Presence of God*   17

1. Be a Pioneer of God's Presence   21

2. Rooted in God's Presence   37

3. Tapping into His Treasure   51

4. Wholehearted Living   65

5. Spheres of Life   79

6. Presence Weapons   93

7. The Throne of His Glory   115

8. Prophets of Intimacy   127

9. The Gravity of His Glory   141

10. Foundational Thinking   155

11. Presence Communities   169

12. Visions of Glory   181

Foreword

Unexpectedly, God's presence filled me completely and powerfully. It was as though liquid love were flooding my sin-sick soul, bringing miraculous and immediate transformation. All shame, guilt and condemnation left immediately. I was instantly aware that I had become pure, clean and new, and that the familiar brooding, lingering darkness I had wrestled with in my heart had been absorbed and dissolved in this amazing "love presence."

I will never forget that experience or that night. It was December 1976, around midnight—the hour I was gloriously born again by the Spirit of God. I was introduced to faith in Jesus Christ through His tangible, life-transforming presence.

Earlier that evening I had attended a neighborhood Bible study hosted by a local Anglican church. When I walked through the door, I encountered a sense of peace that was beyond my understanding. It was undeniably the presence of God, and for some reason I knew it. Never had I encountered peace like that before.

During the meeting, the regulars in the group shared their stories, one by one, of how Jesus had forgiven them their sin and given them a brand-new life. I longed for this new life but did not know if God could love the likes of me. My own sin, I believed, was greater than that of those who had shared. Did God have a limit as to how bad you were permitted to be and still be accepted into His family? If He did have a limit, I had exceeded it, for sure.

I returned home aware of a deep desire to know God but doubting He would accept me. I did not know how to pray or conduct myself in His holy presence. So I found myself collapsing to my knees and crying out with simple words from my heart:

"God, I have nothing to offer You, only my messed-up life. But those people at the Bible study said You forgave them their sin and gave them a new beginning. I'm not sure if You would want to come into my heart or not—but I'd like You to."

I had started to weep halfway through the prayer. I was afraid of His rejection. Yet He did not hesitate to respond to my humble cry. He came into my life that night with such a powerful sense of His presence that I was smitten by His love and have never been the same.

I was birthed in presence. His presence. His glorious love presence. Since that night, I have longed constantly for more, as one taste of Him apprehends you for life and creates a deep desire for more of Him. "O taste and see that the LORD is good" (Psalm 34:8 NASB). He is always with you. He will never leave you or forsake you. And whether you feel Him or not, He is right there all the time.

As I grew in the Lord, I learned to exercise my faith to connect to His tangible presence. I discovered that He manifests various aspects of His being: holiness, healing, peace and glory, to name a few. I was hungry to discover more, yet there were very few resources available at that time on how to access and encounter Him.

My heart leapt, then, when John Belt wrote this book, *The Secret to Experiencing God's Presence*. It will help many who struggle to experience God. John and his wife, Brandi, enjoy God's manifest presence regularly and long for every child of God to know Him in that way.

You are deeply loved and cherished by God, and His desire is that you know and encounter Him—His presence. As He said to Moses, He speaks also to you: "My presence shall go with you, and I will give you rest" (Exodus 33:14 NASB).

You are a passionate pursuer of His presence. That is why you picked up this book. He will not disappoint you. When you seek, you will find. May your journey be filled with joy unspeakable and full of glory as you encounter Him in new ways . . . as you live and abide in His presence.

Dr. Patricia King, founder, Patricia King Ministries;
co-founder, XPmedia.com

Acknowledgments

Thanks to our wonderful God and Father, even Jesus, for pouring His love into my heart, giving me a desire to know Him more and to hunger for His Spirit—and for giving me the most amazing family!

This new offering would not have happened without my beautiful rose of a wife, Brandi, who kept encouraging me, over and over again, to write this book. I am so blessed that you are mine! You are a shining example of selfless sacrifice, resiliency, integrity and faith, as well as a wonderful, loving mother of our boys.

To James and Michal Ann Goll for the years they shared with me. I am so thankful for that great time when I was able to be an intimate part of your life and family. Thank you, James, for sacrificially pouring into my life in so many ways!

I give thanks as well to Jeron Cooper for sowing enormous seeds of joy, faith, hope and love in my life. His family and life were an inspiration to me. He helped to give me the best start in my walk with God—more than anyone could have asked for. Jeron's humorous joy was contagious, love apparent, with encouragement over the top and consistent! I am certain that heaven is an even better place now that he is there.

Introduction

The Essential Presence of God

> And they heard the sound of the LORD God walking
> in the garden in the cool of the day, and Adam and
> his wife hid themselves from the presence of the
> LORD God among the trees of the garden.
>
> Genesis 3:8

At the beginning of Creation, God created a Garden and gave it to mankind, the Garden of Eden. In this Garden, God's intent was for man to live in a perpetual state of communion with Him. And he did. Adam and Eve experienced God's presence continually.

Adam was told not to eat of the Tree of Knowledge of Good and Evil because the result would be spiritual and, eventually, physical death. When Adam and Eve disobeyed God, sin entered, bringing separation from God and the loss of their everyday experience—God's presence. The intimacy with God they once enjoyed was disrupted because of their disobedience. Fear entered their hearts, causing them to hide from God. They were estranged from His presence. From this point on, God spoke prophetically of a day of restoration, when He would once again come into an even greater intimacy with a people who were His very own (see Ezekiel 11:19–20).

Today we can see this same scenario playing out before us. People still hide from God's presence because either they love sin more or they do not understand God's nature—that He actually wants to help them. People still run from the One who loves them most. When we do not see that God is the only One who can help us out, we revert to inferior methods of fixing ourselves. In many cases, people get caught in a pattern of self-help—as did Adam and Eve, whose natural response was to sew fig leaves to cover themselves. God wants to surround us and fill us with His presence. The sacrifice that God made to clothe Adam and Eve (see Genesis 3:21) is a picture of the ultimate provision, Jesus, who has brought us back into the place of intimate fellowship with God.

The Cry of Moses

"And He said, 'My Presence will go with you, and I will give you rest.' Then he said to Him, 'If Your Presence does not go with us, do not bring us up from here'" (Exodus 33:14–15).

God desires us to be a people who know the importance of having His presence with us. We see in Scripture that the presence of God is essential for our lives to have lasting fruit and fulfillment. Moses was brought up in the ways of the Egyptians, raised in the house of Pharaoh, to later find out that he was of Israelite descent. Though Moses left Egypt, God sent him back to deliver the people of Israel. Moses learned that it was only through God's presence abiding with him that he would be able to do what God called him to do. He refused to go without the presence of God. He understood his need for God's presence and rest. This is true for our lives as well; without His presence, there will be no rest and no lasting fruit to show for our efforts.

Moses knew that if God's presence was not with them, they were destined to fail. There is no true success without God's glory in our lives, only a failing imitation of it. We do not want to fool ourselves into thinking that we can do what He is calling us to do in our own strength. Many fail because they have relied on gifting alone, leaving behind an essential component: a life in God's presence.

Indwelling Glory

Look at the Tabernacle, the Temple and the Ark of the Covenant, where the presence of God dwelt. They are pictures, types of how God wants to inhabit His people. In the Old Testament God gave blueprints to Moses for the Tabernacle (which would also house the Ark of the Covenant) so that His manifest presence would be among the people and so that sacrifices could be instituted for their sins. Through this, God revealed the need for sacrifice to cover sin. Now we have access to enter into the holiest of all in the heaven of heavens through the blood of Jesus Christ.

> Therefore, brethren, having boldness to enter the Holiest by the blood of Jesus, by a new and living way which He consecrated for us, through the veil, that is, His flesh, and having a High Priest over the house of God, let us draw near with a true heart in full assurance of faith, having our hearts sprinkled from an evil conscience and our bodies washed with pure water.
>
> Hebrews 10:19–22

A divine exchange takes place as we enter into God's presence. The sacrifice of Jesus makes it possible for us to enter into that true temple in the heavens. Because of this, as we enter into the holiest in the heavens, He also comes to inhabit us in His manifest presence. We have been created to be dwelling places of His Spirit. As we continually welcome the Holy Spirit in our lives, the reality of His presence manifests to us in a tangible way. The cross of Christ has made it possible for us to have the most intimate communion with God through the Person of the Holy Spirit.

Through *The Secret to Experiencing God's Presence*, my hope is that you will discover just how much God wants to have you experience intimacy with Him through His manifested presence; that you will be stirred to seek God with your whole heart; that you will find yourself in the same place as the psalmist David, saying, "LORD, I have loved the habitation of Your house, and the place where Your glory dwells" (Psalm 26:8). Not only this, but I pray that you will come to realize that *you* are that dwelling place of God, the very habitation of His presence.

1

Be a Pioneer of God's Presence

Go through, go through the gates! Prepare the way
for the people; build up, build up the highway! Take
out the stones, lift up a banner for the peoples!

Isaiah 62:10

Not having been raised in a church setting, I committed my life to God at age nineteen in a nondenominational faith church. On Friday nights we met for a Bible study with worship, teaching and a chair in the middle for people to be prayed for. This was a very intimate crowd of about twelve people. The chair saw some memorable moments, as a new person would sit in it just about every weekend. One night it was my turn. People surrounded me, praying for me, while one man ministered "deliverance." They did this using a book on deliverance that listed every possible spirit (demon) you could imagine! The folks in the Bible study just went down the list until something worked.

Because they did not embrace the extremes of deliverance in that book, but just the general idea of helping people get free, they encouraged me to grow in my own personal devotion to the Lord, so as not to become codependent upon them. Many times this is not the case with those who lead deliverance ministries. This happened in the context of a healthy home and family environment. Much of the freedom people experienced was because of the hunger of their own hearts. The method was good, but the desire to be free was the greater element. When we have a willingness to cooperate with God, He will go to whatever lengths necessary to help us. He will even help us in ways that seem to be unorthodox, using things we would not expect Him to use.

During this time I also received the baptism in the Holy Spirit. As I continued to engage with the Holy Spirit, an amazing experience was made available to me, one both dependable and continual in the presence of God. Progressively, as I continued to welcome the Holy Spirit in my life, God began teaching me the value of singing new songs to Him. Through this I began connecting with His presence on a deeper level than I had experienced before. My personal worship times with God continued to develop, for I had discovered a new sound and a place in the Spirit that came like a river of refreshing, which I could access at any time. Up until this time I had been having wonderful experiences in worship, but having songs come from my own heart elevated this to a different level of communion. God wanted to birth something new inside of me. At the time, I did not realize it, but I was pioneering something in my life that did not currently exist.

Does God not issue such invitations to all of us? God loves to "add" something new to our lives—something helpful, something of His presence that changes us. It takes willingness on our end to take those first steps before we can see the fruit of it in our lives. But as we move forward, we begin to see more clearly the work that God is doing within us. We are ushering something new into an empty place. God was creating a hunger inside me for more of Him. As I grew, God gave me more and more of a vision for a people who would be passionate for the presence of God, with hearts willing to pay the price to see His glory.

In every generation people emerge who are passionate about something, so much so that they are willing to pay whatever cost necessary to see a vision come to pass. Pioneering takes that kind of passion, and a passionate person will pay the price. Pioneers are people who can no longer conform to the typical pattern of things accepted. Many times they take a direction contrary to the trend in culture or society. They choose not to tolerate the accepted norm any longer because of a greater vision burning inside of them. For these people, change is not an option; change is a *must*. They have been entrusted with visions of something better, of things that have yet to be seen.

Where does this kind of pioneering passion meet the modern-day prophets of change? It all begins with your heart being saturated with His Spirit. When you are passionate about a particular thing, it becomes your entire world. At your foundation, God wants you to be passionate about Him—even His presence. Are you willing to be a pioneer so that a greater realm of His presence may be established in the earth? As your devotional life grows in Him, you will become a conduit of His glory to the world.

In the private place of devotion, God's desires are deposited within you. Desires, dreams and visions are birthed inside, catapulting you to a place where you become passionate enough to pay the price for the thing God has awakened inside of you. While some are content to do things in the usual way, pioneers cannot succumb to the current order of things. Such is the state of the heart when you are in passionate pursuit of God.

The Challenges of Pioneers

Pioneers typically do not get the popular vote, for they are not around to entertain what is popular or to follow trends. John the Baptist was the voice of one crying in the desert. He knew the lonely place of following after God to prepare the way for the Lord Himself. Some did respect him, but how many really wanted to be his buddy?

And what about Jesus? Though He had twelve in His inner circle, only three were especially close to Him. Even His disciples questioned Him. At one point His disciple base had grown to seventy, but then Jesus gave a tough teaching: "You must eat my flesh and drink my blood" (see John 6:56). His group slimmed back down to the original twelve. At the height of persecution, they all left Him.

> From that time many of His disciples went back and walked with Him no more. Then Jesus said to the twelve, "Do you also want to go away?" But Simon Peter answered Him, "Lord, to whom shall we go? You have the words of eternal life. Also we have come to believe and know that You are the Christ, the Son of the living God."
>
> John 6:66–69

Pioneers face much opposition because they go against the grain of common thought. Jesus was constantly assaulted by the religious leaders of His day. They called Him demon possessed, a deceiver and a false prophet. Paul was imprisoned and beaten, suffering greatly for pioneering the Gospel of Christ. Jesus' response to this kind of persecution was, in layman's terms, "Don't be surprised. If they did it to Me, they will also do it to you." Opposition is just part of following God.

How does that apply to us today? We must make sure that we are not creating a candy-coated version of the Gospel that caters to our own selfish gratification. The majority of people in our society are hooked on fast food, the big event, the Big Mac and the Big Gulp. If it is not big, it cannot possibly have relevance or impact, right? But here was Jesus, with only twelve disciples, and one of them was there just to betray Him.

Understand that Jesus was the Son of God with power and signs, wonders and miracles following Him. No ministry on earth would ever compare to the glory and power that He walked in; yet He only had twelve. He only had eleven truly committed to Him. That does not mean God is not in big things, but beware of underestimating what looks insignificant. Do that and you will miss Jesus. He told us the road that leads to destruction is wide, and it is a popular one: "Enter by the narrow gate; for wide is the gate and broad is the way that leads to destruction, and there are many who go in by it. Because narrow is the gate and difficult is the way which leads to life, and there are few who find it" (Matthew 7:13–14). In other words, in the world's eyes, bigger is better. This is not to discredit moves of the Spirit like that in Acts 2, in which three thousand people came to be added to the Church in a day. Nations will be born, and are being born, in a day (see Isaiah 66:8). Still, there is a personal price we pay to come into these windows of glory.

Following Christ will cost you. While anything good costs something, following Jesus costs everything. He is the One who determines the price each of us pays as we follow Him. Our desire should be to have a life that God can fill and use.

Here is a small story, but it is my story. Maybe you have one similar to it. When I began writing soaking music, I had no support. For those who are not familiar with it, "soaking music" is a genre of music that came out of a wave of revival in the 1990s that facilitated prayer in the presence of God. At that time, no one was encouraging me to do it. My talent was not all that great; I could barely play the keyboard. Some would say I was not good at all. I probably would have agreed with that assessment. After all, I lived in Nashville, Tennessee, a city full of excellent musicians and talented people. What would I have to offer?

But inside of me was a sound that I had to do something with. That sound was created in me through my own devotional life with God—something most people did not have. It was the "God factor." Even though my first project did not impress many, God opened the doors. Now I have created more than thirty music projects in just fifteen years. I was pioneering a sound that would create an atmosphere for devotional life in the presence of God. What was the price I had to pay? It was ignoring what others thought and the opinions of men and going against the grain of that unseen, spiritual resistance. Is that not what Jesus dealt with? The resistance of those saying, "You're just a carpenter. You're from Nazareth—can anything good come from there?" This is the everyday stuff that all of us have to face and choose to turn the other direction. It is where the rubber meets the road in our lives.

Pioneers Who Came Before

Pioneers clear the path, working the ground to open the way for future generations. They have a vision beyond themselves. Though God has a plan for each of our lives, we need to understand that we should not have a self-serving vision but one that helps others discover the place in God's plan for their lives. One of many definitions of the word *pioneer* is one who ventures into unknown or unclaimed territory to settle. A pioneer can also be a person or group that originates or helps open up a new line of thought or activity—which could also be described as "one of the first to settle in a territory."

Maria Woodworth-Etter, who lived in the second half of the 1800s and into the early 1900s, was a pioneer of her day who brought the power and presence of God to countless people. She traveled across the nation, from Massachusetts to California, holding revival meetings continually for years on end. In her day, transportation was primitive; Maria saw the shift from most people journeying by horse and buggy to the automobile becoming an important means of travel. Today we can fly around the world in a single day, whereas for her it took weeks to travel from one side of the nation to the other. It is amazing to think that such glory was poured out here in America not so long ago. In this quote from her book *Signs and Wonders*, Maria expressed the price she was paying, as well as the faithfulness of God:

> It is over fourteen years since I started out to stand between the living and the dead, to point sinners to the Lamb of God that taketh away the sins of the world. I have been going from one battlefield to another almost day and night. During this time I have travelled about thirty-five thousand three hundred and twenty-two miles, and held meetings in thirteen States; have stood before hundreds of thousands. The power of the Holy Ghost has gone out from these meetings all over the United States, and been felt in many places across the mighty deep in awakening power.*

I recall a dream I had about Maria Woodworth-Etter years ago in which she was standing with her right hand lifted. In this encounter she was covered in the iridescent mist of God's glory. I woke up in the presence of God feeling amazement at the glory of God upon this lady's life. The Lord gave me this vision to increase my hunger to see His glory come. God is looking for a generation to be caught up in the wonder of His glory so as to carry His glory and power in such a way today.

Joining Maria Woodworth-Etter have been other pioneers of God's presence who knew their desperate need for it. Kathryn

---

*Maria Woodworth-Etter, *Signs and Wonders God Wrought in the Ministry for Forty Years Including Prophesies, Visions, Healings, and Sermons*, abridged ed. (Hants, U.K.: Revival Library, n.d., originally published 1918), 57, https://www.scribd.com/doc/201880506/Signs-and-Wonders-by-Maria-Woodworth-Etter.

Kuhlman, William Branham and Aimee Semple McPherson are just a few of the ones who followed God with an unreserved passion—joining the psalmist's heart cry in Psalm 42:1–2: "As the deer pants for the water brooks, so pants my soul for You, O God. My soul thirsts for God, for the living God. When shall I come and appear before God?"

Kathryn Kuhlman was a healing evangelist who was passionately in touch with the reality of the Holy Spirit. She embodied a life lived in the most intimate relationship with the Spirit. William Branham was a prophetic healing evangelist who had notable signs and wonders in his ministry that accompanied very detailed and accurate prophetic visions, words and encounters. Aimee Semple McPherson used the dramatics of theatrics in the flow of the Holy Spirit, and people would receive miraculous healings as a result. We also see biblical examples of those who knew the presence of God, many of them described as prophets. This is the common denominator in the lives of Enoch, Abraham, Samuel, David, Elijah and others.

Taken by God

Enoch, the great-grandfather of Noah, is one of my favorite Bible figures. That may be because, even though very little is said about him, what is said about him is what I would want to be said about me. "Enoch walked with God after he fathered Methuselah 300 years and had other sons and daughters. Thus all the days of Enoch were 365 years. *Enoch walked with God, and he was not, for God took him*" (Genesis 5:22–24 ESV, emphasis added).

A beautiful picture emerges from the simple details of Enoch's life. He lived 365 years; this symbolizes "completeness," for it correlates to the completion of a year, which is 365 days. This number represents a full cycle. Then we read this statement:

"He was not, for God took him." What a note on Enoch's life! It seems that God loved Enoch so much that He would rather have Enoch with Him as good company in heaven.

The book of Jude quotes Enoch in verses 14–15, a quotation that comes not from the Bible but rather from the book of Enoch. The book of Enoch was attributed as Scripture in the epistle of Barnabas and by many of the early Church fathers, such as Athenagoras, Clement of Alexandria, Irenaeus and Tertullian, who wrote that the book of Enoch had been rejected by the Jews because it contained prophecies pertaining to Christ. Although we do not regard this book as having the same authority as the 66 books that are part of the sealed canon of Scripture, it is a very interesting read that reveals that Enoch was most definitely a prophet, someone who lived very close to the heart of God. In it we find not only references to Christ but a more detailed account of the flood, the origin of demons and some possible insights on how there came to be giants in the land (referred to in the book of Genesis). In his day Enoch was undoubtedly a forerunner and a man who had learned to live in the presence of God.

Lessons from Abraham

We have one of the best examples of someone who truly lived the life of a pioneer in Abraham. Abraham ventured out not knowing where he was going but simply following the voice of God. God gave Abraham amazing promises that would be obtained completely by faith. With all that Abraham went through, all of the work and sacrifice, if God had shown him in advance all that was involved—the journey, the length of time to obtain the promises, the challenges, the fights and the heart-wrenching call to sacrifice Isaac (albeit with God providing the sacrifice)—he might not have done it. Is it not the same with us?

God gives us lofty promises but hides the price tag. Oh, we know it is going to cost something. If we have any understanding, we know there will be a price—just not what that price will be. In His goodness He spares us the details, for He knows the best way for us to live is one step at a time.

> Now the LORD had said to Abram: "Get out of your country, from your family and from your father's house, to a land that I will show you. I will make you a great nation; I will bless you and make your name great; and you shall be a blessing. I will bless those who bless you, and I will curse him who curses you; and in you all the families of the earth shall be blessed."
>
> Genesis 12:1–3

What can we learn from this true example of the pioneering spirit?

1. The Familiar Was Removed

When God is ready to do something fresh in our lives, many times He will have us leave that which is familiar. In this process He is tearing down many of the mindsets that we have embraced through association. God is building a new foundation in our thinking to prepare us for the better things that He has in store.

I was born and raised in Oklahoma City, Oklahoma, in the heartland of the United States. Compared to other cities, it is like a town in size. I can remember, just out of high school, leaving my familiar surroundings to go to a place I had never been before. It was exciting; I did not know what to expect, but I was embarking on an adventure. Where you grow up is full of your history, the good, the bad and the ugly. And, yes, there was good, there was bad, there was even some ugly.

Much later in my life, my mother told me I was a very unhappy kid growing up. She had never said that before, and I was surprised to hear it. But I do remember ups and downs entwined with much ridicule and shame. Looking back, I feel as if I am looking at a completely different person, someone I do not even know, because the transformation in me was so radical and quick. God apparently saved the best for last in Oklahoma City, because I found the Lord and was filled with His Spirit at the very end of my days there. Sadness turned to joy and confusion to peace when I gave my life to Jesus. It was then that I realized that the best thing for me was to move to a new place, a place where I could rebuild my life the right way in the Lord. This also helped me get away from the things that represented the old life. After a year I set out on a journey, leaving Oklahoma for a completely new and unfamiliar place. My entire identity shifted to the new person I was in this new land.

God has amazing adventures for us. He prods us out of the known into the unknown, for that is where our faith thrives. If everything is common and familiar, there is no adventure; we can walk by our own understanding and sight in a limited little box. God is the ultimate box breaker, breaking us out of the little boxes we create. They are illusionary safe places that are not safe at all. They only give the façade of safety, when in reality they are cold, sterile, limited and boring.

Get out of the box with God and live a little. Step out of the boat of comfort onto the waters of faith, and watch God work His wonders before your eyes!

2. Codependency Was Broken

God did not only move Abraham geographically; He separated Abraham from his family. This may well have been a huge move for him. In that culture and time, it was sacred to keep families together. God wants to break us out of every codependency so we will learn to be solely dependent on Him. Are there people you have codependent relationships with? Challenge yourself to move out of those kinds of relationships. Create some wise boundaries. Do not sever the relationship, but use wisdom and create some distance.

Some time back, my wife, Brandi, had a dream about some people she knew who turned into leeches. She woke up the next morning ready for a fresh body cleanse. This was an allegorical vision of people with codependent spirits who were unknowingly sucking out life and strength. Not a pretty picture, but rather revealing in how people close to us can justify all kinds of actions, not realizing the true motives of their hearts. For a long time I have said that if you knew you were deceived, then you wouldn't be.

3. God Prepared a New Place

"By faith Abraham obeyed when he was called to go out to the place which he would receive as an inheritance. And he went out, not knowing where he was going" (Hebrews 11:8).

Abraham was willing to move without any details of where he was going to end up. God promised to bless Abraham but did not give him all the specifics. It takes a desperate heart to fuel personal sacrifice, leaving the old things behind, to follow God into the unknown and unfamiliar. This is how God works with us. He gives us a promise, but He leaves the response in our court.

Without our personal sacrifice of leaving things behind, God will have a hard time taking us into something new. It is a good thing to embrace change. God is always changing us, challenging us and making us a better reflection of His image. Only by following Him can we discover the new lands that He has for us.

I went through a season in my life of downsizing. Before it really started, God reminded me of the story that Jesus shared about the camel going through the eye of a needle (see Matthew 19:24). For a camel to fit through the needle, much has to be unloaded and left behind. I was getting rid of things left and right over a period of almost four years. In the process I started to realize just how much stuff I had accumulated. As I realized how much of the stuff I did not even use and what it represented, I had no problem getting rid of it. That time of downsizing brought me to what I actually used and needed. Other things needed to go because of what they represented from my past—an old season or an association something was connected with. Once that season of purging was over, I could rebuild in wisdom, investing the right way. It was all about crossing over into a new place. "Behold, I will do a new thing, now it shall spring forth; shall you not know it?" (Isaiah 43:19).

4. Obedience Comes with Promises

In Genesis 12:1–3, God gave Abraham incredible promises for his obedience. We find that God gives us conditional promises that require action from us. We can break it down this way: *If we do our part in following His voice, He will do His part in blessing our lives.* Just as an earthly father gives rewards to his own children, so our Father in heaven is the Rewarder in our lives as we put Him first. Here are God's blessings for our obedience:

- I will make of you a great nation.
- I will bless you.
- I will make your name great.
- You will be a blessing.
- I will bless those who bless you, and curse him who curses you.
- In you all families of the earth will be blessed.

5. It Is Never Too Late!

"So Abram departed as the Lord had spoken to him, and Lot went with him. And Abram was seventy-five years old when he departed from Haran" (Genesis 12:4). Abram was 75 years old before he even left! He was 90 when he had Isaac. That should show all of us that it is *never too late* to get in on what God wants to do. God puts notes in between the lines of these stories to encourage us to stay the course, keep the faith and believe in His faithfulness.

There is a price that we have to pay—things we need to leave behind and a resetting of vision that needs to take place—for us to walk into the place of promise God has for us. Abraham was, after all, 75 years old. What if he had decided to stay where he was? It seems that God created desperation in Abraham to get him out of that place. God moved him out of a place of barrenness to a place of promise and hope.

Just as with Abraham, God has a way of preparing us for new seasons to bring us into a new place. Somehow this man had discovered God and God had discovered him. Maybe there was an "unsettled" quality in Abraham yearning for something more than what he had. No doubt the breeze of God's presence was blowing upon him, creating unrest to make Abraham ready and willing to follow God's voice.

Has God Rocked Your Boat?

Have you grown discontent in the boat of your life, in your current state? Are you ready to break out into a new place, to find a new freedom? God has a way of making us ready for something better, something greater than we are. He has a way of using the circumstances of life to create a hunger. The challenges of life can be overwhelming, but God wants to use those things to create desperation, to the point that we reach deeper and higher for Him.

God uses the various circumstances of our lives as a way of bringing us to a place where we will pursue Him—placing all of our hope in Him. He has a plan, and He wants you to be a part of it. Allow Him to change your life and fill your life with His presence. God is not looking for extraordinary vessels. He uses ordinary people who make themselves available to Him. We each "prepare the way for the Lord" to come in our hearts, so that He would use us in extraordinary ways.

God's Glory through Us

"For the earth will be filled with the knowledge of the glory of the LORD, as the waters cover the sea" (Habakkuk 2:14).

God is looking for those who are willing to pay the price for His glory on earth. When we gather together, His manifest presence and glory should be with us. For Scripture says that the earth shall be filled with the knowledge of the glory of the Lord, as the waters cover the sea. This will happen no other way except that His glory is made manifest in the midst of His people, the Church.

We are "living stones," the habitation of God (see 1 Peter 2:5). As more corporate expressions of His glory are birthed and established, there will be an exponential increase of exposure to the hungry and thirsty who have not known or experienced God's presence. It is His presence that satisfies, His presence that fills us and leads us.

My prayer is that God will so stir your heart that you will embrace a heart to be a pioneer who will make His presence known. As you learn to live life with God, your perceptions of who He is and how He interacts with us are foundational for you to grow healthy and strong.

Life Application

- **ASK** God for a greater passion for His presence. Everything we are, everything we have and all that we are able to accomplish are by His grace.

- **WELCOME** the Holy Spirit to bring freshness of intimacy and revelation in your life. God is always waiting for us to initiate. He is ready and willing to pour out His Spirit.

- **ALLOW** the Lord to show you how to get out of the boat of limitations and to take you into a place of expanse in His presence. With God are no limitations; we are only limited by our limited perceptions of who He is, not grasping His fervent desire to bring us into greater experience with Him.

- **REALIZE** that you are a vessel that God desires to inhabit, to fill with His presence. God has favorites, and you are one of them! The sooner you realize this, the sooner you will begin to experience His love and presence. Faith is the magnet that draws God to us.

2

Rooted in God's Presence

Beloved, let us love one another, for love is of God;
and everyone who loves is born of God and knows
God. He who does not love does not know God,
for God is love.

1 John 4:7–8

As you learn to live in the presence of God, realize that
sometimes the simple things He teaches you can have the
biggest impact on your life. Revelation, both in foundational
truth and personal wisdom, establishes us. Our basic perceptions
of God and our foundational thinking as believers determine the
way we live. Our perception of God is the central engine that
determines how we approach Him and present Him to others.
If we have a faulty view of who He is and what He is like, then
we will pass on a distorted picture of His nature to others.

Our Perceptions of God

One of the first things we need to understand is that God is
love. His love is what motivates Him to do the things He does.

He is not trying to prove a point to us or make a grand display; He is wholly moved by His love for us.

Growing up, I essentially had no grid for God. I had good parents who did not raise me in church. That can be a good thing (in any case, God made a good thing out of it). But my granddad had a maid, a sweet black woman who had been around as long as I could remember, named Inez. We called her Iny. She would always sing the song "Jesus Loves Me" to my brother and me. That was the seed, planted in me from a very young age, that I credit for coming to know Jesus.

Outside of Iny and a few positive associations with Jesus, I was not taught about God. Just knowing the one song, "Jesus Loves Me," was enough for me to at least know that He was approachable. But, still, not knowing Him made God very much a mystery. My brother and I grew up in a house with a basement that served as a final resting place for lots of books and stuff, all gathering dust. Among the other forgotten items was one gigantic Bible. We would look upon it as if it were a long-lost scroll, full of great mysteries. All of this shaped a mysterious perception of God in my mind.

One day, after having been in relationship with God a few years, I lay on the floor in my prayer time, feeling broken. I was crying out to God that I might know Him in a deeper way. As I sprawled on the floor, I stared at the ceiling of the room, saying, "God, I've experienced you as Jesus and the Holy Spirit, but not as Father." At that moment I felt an amazing love come into the room. It was a deeper and more personal experience than I had encountered up to that point. Something was added to me that day, a fresh encounter with a different face of His being. My view of God was altered, shifting my day from cloudy to sunshine. He gave me a download of His Father's heart of love and goodness. When we experience encounters with God like this, the eyes of our hearts are opened to Him in new and fresh ways.

Because of His love, He demonstrates His goodness. It is the goodness of God that brings us to repentance, not the gavel of judgment. Jesus did not come to condemn the world but that through Him the world would be saved. Years ago I heard one pastor summarize, with great humor, one of the basic tenets of the faith: "God good, devil bad." That is the truth. If the Church could just get this down, we would experience a major reformation in our thinking.

Another facet of God's nature that cannot be compromised is that He is holy. Sin cannot exist in God's presence. His holiness will annihilate the presence of sin. Heaven itself is completely separate from sinners; only saints dwell in heaven. Just as we need to embrace His love, His goodness and His righteousness, we need to lay hold of His holiness.

The Doorway of Faith

Other perception issues lie in our understanding of the basics of our walk with God. What does it look like? What is to be the foundational norm? When we enter the Kingdom of God, we come with faith as of a child. Faith is not a state of having everything figured out; it is leaning on the Holy Spirit. The natural mind is always trying to have the upper hand, but Jesus came to help us live from a superior place. He put a new spirit inside of us that is created in the image and likeness of God.

One thing Jesus accomplished for us is the ability to change who is in the driver's seat. Even then, it is still up to us to choose to live out of the new creation that He has made us to be. Struggles and long journeys of trying to connect with the Lord originate in our natural minds. Faith, on the other hand, is simple. It is our entry pass. Anything connected with our works and our own personal effort will not get us through the door into God's presence. God is looking at the work of His Son, not our works.

Through my own personal experience, I have learned that whatever we try to produce outside of a life of intimate communion with God almost always fails or becomes a laborious struggle. We can have a lot of good ideas—maybe even some God ideas—but even our ideas come out of our intimate life with Him. If we lose that intimacy, we lose our connection to the power outlet that enables our plans to be successful. Abiding in Christ creates a living faith that works in our lives.

Many things we do not need to fully understand but rather accept by faith. "For as the heavens are higher than the earth, so are My ways higher than your ways, and My thoughts than your thoughts" (Isaiah 55:9). As we lay our natural efforts down, we embrace the work of the cross of Christ. Here we will experience breakthrough in our lives as we interact with God's Spirit and presence.

Life over Law

As an example of how the natural mind works against the purposes of God, let's consider the scenario of someone in imminent danger of losing his or her life. The normal, natural response is to try to rescue the person as quickly as possible. Laws lose their application when a life is at stake. If the law says that we cannot speed on the road, but we see someone who needs emergency help, we will ignore that law, breaking it to save the person's life. If this is not our reaction, we have become legalistic. Love and life are greater than laws. Under Hitler's reign during World War II, it was illegal to hide Jewish people, but they would break that law to save lives, because it had an evil intent. The motive of our hearts is the most important issue.

In the book of Acts we see how the religious leaders persecuted the early Church, commanding them not to speak in the name of Jesus or to teach in His name. Here is another very clear picture of man-made laws that are inferior to the plans of God. God's plan is for all to come to the saving knowledge of Jesus Christ. Any law that prevents this is made to be broken, because life trumps law.

> And when they had brought them, they set them before the council. And the high priest asked them, saying, "Did we not strictly command you not to teach in this name? And look, you have filled Jerusalem with your doctrine, and intend to bring this Man's blood on us!" But Peter and the other apostles answered and said: "We ought to obey God rather than men."
>
> Acts 5:27–29

When law fails to protect life or give life, then it must go, because our obedience to God is never to be compromised. The natural mind, having everything "figured out," tells you that you are supposed to obey the law. But if someone is in a life-or-death situation, even though you might technically break a law in order to help, the right thing to do is to help the person—to save that person's life.

Saving a person's life is the natural thing to do. It does not work that way in toxic religion, though; all "normal" thinking goes out the window. People who are religious become experts at doing everything perfectly and legally right, while squashing, hurting and even killing not only their own lives but other people's spiritual lives. Such was the case in Jesus' day:

> But the ruler of the synagogue answered with indignation, because Jesus had healed on the Sabbath; and he said to the crowd, "There are six days on which men ought to work; therefore come and be healed on them, and not on the Sabbath day." The Lord then answered him and said, "Hypocrite! Does not each one of you on the Sabbath loose his ox or donkey from the stall, and lead it away to water it? So ought not this woman, being a

daughter of Abraham, whom Satan has bound—think of it—
for eighteen years, be loosed from this bond on the Sabbath?"

Luke 13:14–16

The synagogue rulers were venomously angry with Jesus because He was not following the laws that they held dear. Jesus exalted life above law, offending the natural thinking of these leaders. When we have everything figured out, this is a prime opportunity for God to slay our sacred cows. And He will.

What sacred cows do you have in your life that masquerade as coming from God but are really man-made? Do you have expectations of others that are in reality your own and not what God requires? Is God's love your method for bringing people closer to Him, or is laying down the law? God has not called us to be executioners but followers who help others experience the reality of His love. It is the goodness of God that brings transformation. When people experience the Lord's goodness, a hunger is created inside their hearts for more of Him.

Holiness: Our Heavenly Origins

Holiness has been much misunderstood. It has become the kind of subject that people would rather brush under the carpet in order to embrace an unbiblical view of grace. Living a holy life does not fit with today's "everything goes" mentality. Many would associate holiness with some exterior acts of humility—a self-absorbed life rather than an inward devotion in the presence of God.

To get past this, we first need to understand what holiness is not. Holiness is not how we dress; it is not about how we look on the outside but rather on the inside. Holiness is not mean or grumpy. God is not holding a gavel over our heads, waiting to slam it down the moment we make a mistake; that is condemnation, not holiness. A holy life can be created in us only through the life substance of God's Spirit within us. God calls us to live from the inside out, not the outside in. Someone may look perfect and clean on the outside but be filthy on the inside. Holiness is realized as we learn to walk with the Holy Spirit. It is He who transforms us through the welcoming of His presence inside of us. Holiness is a beautiful core aspect in the nature of God.

Andrew Murray, someone who is best known today for his devotional writings, placed great emphasis on the need for a rich, personal devotional life. Here he comments on the need for the beauty of holiness in the believer's life:

> Now this is just the condition of many believers. They are converted; they know what it is to have assurance and faith; they believe in pardon for sin; they begin to work for God; and yet, somehow, there is very little growth in spirituality, in the real heavenly life. We come into contact with them, and we feel at once there is something wanting; there is none of the beauty of holiness or of the power of God's Spirit in them. This is the condition of the carnal Corinthians, expressed in what was said to the Hebrews: "You have had the Gospel so long that by this time you ought to be teachers, and yet you need that men should teach you the very rudiments of the oracles of God."*

"Give to the LORD the glory due His name," 1 Chronicles 16:29 tells us. "Bring an offering, and come before Him. Oh, worship the LORD in the beauty of holiness!" We need to understand that holiness is central to who God is. To be holy is to be *set apart* for God's divine purposes. We should have the kind of faith that makes us want to be holy and set apart for God's purposes. All believers in Jesus Christ are called "saints," which means "holy ones" (see Colossians 1:12). To ignore holiness is to ignore the nature of God and a core part of who we are as followers of Jesus.

---

*Andrew Murray, *The Master's Indwelling* (Radford, Va.: Wilder Publications, 2008), 7.

Holiness is something of a two-sided coin. On one side, we are responsible for our actions. *Responsible* is another unpopular term in our day. Yet we are called to be responsible for living lives worthy of the Lord. Peter writes God's declaration, "Be holy, for I am holy" (1 Peter 1:16). For this, we need understanding. We need to know what is important to God, how we should act and what is pleasing to Him.

The other side of the coin is the "how," or the approach we take to walking in holiness. This side of the coin is where people can slip up and fall into a life of legalism. The method we use in approaching a holy life makes all the difference: We are not called to live by a list but by the indwelling of the *Holy* Spirit. As Paul wrote, "The grace of the Lord Jesus Christ, and the love of God, and the communion of the Holy Spirit be with you all. Amen" (2 Corinthians 13:14). The key for us to live holy lives is to know Him who is holy, to live in communion with the Holy Spirit. It is not by observance of a list but by the indwelling of a person. The Word of God provides us with the understanding, wisdom and knowledge of God that is to be married with the Holy Spirit.

Apart from the Spirit we have only the dry letter. With the Spirit we gain revelation, the light of God that opens our eyes to live out God's will and purposes for our lives. We cannot expect to walk in holiness apart from the Holy Spirit. Holiness is the outward-shining ray from the very Person of God, just as Jesus radiates the Father's glory (see Hebrews 1:3; the word *radiate* in Greek means "brightness," a shining forth of light coming from a luminous body).

When we understand holiness in the context of communion with God, it takes on a different look. Intimacy with God is the foundation for us to be able to be what God has called us to be. Jesus Himself could do nothing apart from the Father: "Then Jesus answered and said to them, 'Most assuredly, I say to you, the Son can do nothing of Himself, but what He sees the Father do; for whatever He does, the Son also does in like manner'" (John 5:19). Jesus had a divine union with God that empowered Him to fulfill the Father's will during His time on earth. His works had the support of all of heaven's resources.

Washed by the Holy Spirit

On one occasion I had a dream in which I heard the angels singing over me, "Holy, holy, holy is the Lord of Hosts, and the angels all bow, crying, 'Holy! Holy!' And the angels all bow . . ."

I woke up from the dream with these words repeating within my heart and the weighty, manifested presence of God upon me. I was struck by the awe of God as I rested in His presence after this encounter. I have had many dreams like this in which God drops a song in my spirit. What does it do? It awakens me to the reality of who He is. It is God saying, *I AM HERE!* Through this encounter the reality of God's presence was released; it was like being washed in His heavenly river.

When we seek God, He rewards us by walking into our lives in powerful ways. If you say that you want God to be real and tangible in your life, I will tell you that God wants it much more than you do! God deposits His reality and life in us through these kinds of experiences. Encounters like this are "instant downloads," things that we could never attain through years and years of study. Study alone will never have the same impact on our lives that one radical, life-changing encounter with God will.

This is how God touches us. The Holy Spirit refreshes, washes and renews us through His presence in our lives. When we engage with the Holy Spirit, He constantly washes and refreshes us to fulfill the plans in the heart of God.

"Not by works of righteousness which we have done, but according to His mercy He saved us, through the washing of

45

regeneration and renewing of the Holy Spirit" (Titus 3:5). We are revived in the presence of the Holy Spirit. He cleanses us from the things of this world that come through our daily interactions. That is why it is so important that we learn to continually drink from the well of His Spirit, as it is written, "Therefore with joy you will draw water from the wells of salvation" (Isaiah 12:3).

Going without water for extended periods is hard on our bodies. Dryness and dehydration cause physical problems. For our spiritual well-being, we need to drink of the Holy Spirit to be spiritually vivacious, alive, having energy to do all God calls us to do. Drinking of the Holy Spirit is absolutely necessary to our spiritual health.

When Jesus met with the woman at the well, He told her that He would give her drink that would spring up to eternal life. She essentially said, "Give me this water, that I may never have to drink again!" Jesus is the eternal, never-ending water source for our lives. He has provided His Holy Spirit for us so that we will not burn out.

The Kingdom of God is marked by an element of simplicity that we cannot afford to lose in our lives. If we lose simplicity, we lose life. To be filled with the Spirit, to be washed by the Spirit, to allow times of refreshing to come to our lives is essential if we are to have any longevity for the purposes of God. Religious activity will dry us up quicker than anything. If we do not continue in meaningful communion with God, we will be left empty, dry and discouraged.

Cleansed by His Word

One day I was listening to an audio recording of a Billy Sunday sermon from the early 1900s. Billy played baseball for National League teams in the 1880s as a popular outfielder; then, in the

1890s, he became a relentless preacher of the Gospel and a significant American evangelist during the first two decades of the twentieth century. It is amazing to listen to the strength of his preaching, because he did not water down the Word of God to the degree it has been watered down today.

Sunday lived in a different time and culture, and he had a particular zeal to turn back the tide of liquor consumption in the United States. His most famous sermon was "Get on the Water Wagon," which he preached many times with great emotion and a "mountain of economic and moral evidence." Sunday is quoted as declaring, "I am the sworn, eternal and uncompromising enemy of the liquor traffic. I have been, and will go on, fighting that damnable, dirty, rotten business with all the power at my command."*

I somewhat cringe at the approach the man had, but I understand that what was culturally accepted was quite different back then. Yet Sunday was speaking as a prophet to society, not only to the Church. He also came from a religious culture that was far different from what exists today and was much more accepted then than it would be now.

That being said, the bar of what is accepted now, with the extreme "sloppy grace" messages that are communicated these days, is somewhat disgraceful. I am a huge believer in the grace of God. But this grace He has given us is not a license to sin; on the contrary, it gives us the power to overcome. There have been abuses in the teaching of holiness that have actually fostered a legalistic expression. We have to set these aside. We need to remember that God is holy. This message is constant throughout the Bible, and there is a reason the Spirit He has given us is called the *Holy* Spirit.

*Billy Sunday, "Get on the Water Wagon," Milestone Documents, accessed December 20, 2017, https://www.milestonedocuments.com/documents/view/billy-sunday-get-on-the-water-wagon/text.

How important is God's Word in our lives? It is our standard. It is the cleansing agent for our lives. I like to use the analogy of detergent and water: The Word of God is like the detergent you use to wash your clothes. When the Word is combined with the Spirit, cleansing occurs. With that in mind, think about the ratio of water to detergent; you should have much more water than detergent. Why? Otherwise your clothes will itch you to the point you go crazy. It is the Holy Spirit who makes the Word alive. It is not really about the quantity of the Word in you but the consistency. We should, however, strive to have a steady diet of both.

"Great peace have they which love thy law: and nothing shall offend them" (Psalm 119:165 KJV). Hiding His Word in our hearts and embracing the Spirit bring a fullness of what God desires for us. Some believers are more focused on the Word; others are more enamored with the Holy Spirit. We need extreme levels of both the Word and the Spirit to live in God's fullness.

Walking as New Creations

We are new creations in Christ. Carnality is the way of the world, which is attuned to the cravings of the flesh, sensual desires and self-focus. Carnal Christians have not quite disconnected from the spirit of the world. What an inferior way to live when Christ paid the highest price for us. Living as saints means we are living in the reality of what God has made us to be—new creations with new desires.

When I first started my journey living to please God, I had choices to make. The devil is always faithful to bring you temptation to draw you back into the mess you were in. I can remember making a commitment to God to live radically for Him. All my worldly music went in the trash, what I watched on television changed and all the things that go with making a radical life change shifted. Then someone from my previous life invited me back into the life of worldly pursuits. Here was my moment of truth. Would I go with him to do the things that represented my shameful past, or would I stay in the blessed place that God had provided for me? Our lives are composed of good and bad choices, but some choices are bigger than others. In this instance I made the right choice to invite him into my new world of faith in God instead. He turned down the invitation, and I never saw him again. That was almost thirty years ago.

There are crossroads, times of change in your life when you have to choose a different path, radically different. You are the captain of your life. You alone have control of the rudder of your ship. You have the power of choice. Make radical choices to follow God with your whole heart. Do not play the fence, but instead jump into the river of His presence, where His goodness will overtake you.

Life Application

- **REALIZE** that your spirit man is the center where communion with the Holy Spirit occurs. Submit your will to the heart of God by allowing the Holy Spirit to be your leader.

- **TAKE** a test of how much your natural mind is getting in the way of God: Are you more prone to living by rules and laws, or are you living out of a place of communion with God, where He guides your decisions?

- **WHAT** is your experience in regard to religious life? Do you feel weighed down with all the things you need to do, or do you feel liberated in the abundant life Jesus paid for you to experience?

- **PURSUE** a life that has both the rock of God's Word and the water of the Holy Spirit. The detergent of God's Word and the water of God's Spirit work together to form our thinking after Christ's image.

3

Tapping into His Treasure

> But we have this treasure in earthen vessels, that
> the excellence of the power may be of God and
> not of us.
>
> 2 Corinthians 4:7

What do you value the most? What do you treasure in your heart? When Jesus began His earthly ministry, the heavens opened at His baptism and the Holy Spirit came down in the form of a dove, resting upon Him. After this, the Holy Spirit led Him into the wilderness to be tempted by the devil. His integrity and heart were put to the test, revealing His unwavering resolve and dependence on the Father. He came back in the power and anointing of the Spirit. Jesus valued the will of His Father more than anything else. Because of this He was clothed and filled with God's glory, the treasure of heaven. Even before the cross, Jesus paid a price for the treasure of God's presence and power to be revealed. He wants this same experience of God's presence to abide in us as well. If you want

51

to change your life, then learn how to tap into the reality of the Holy Spirit.

Life Preparation

We have spiritual clothing just as we have natural clothing. We need to be clothed in the presence of God. Many just believe on Jesus, then run around spiritually naked the rest of their lives. We have to make a choice to be clothed in God's presence. It does not just happen because we are now Christians. As our own kids have to learn to put on their clothes, so we have to learn how to clothe ourselves in God's presence.

How does this happen? By committing our lives to spending time in intimate fellowship with Him, allowing His Word in our hearts. When we go without these disciplines in our lives, we walk around spiritually naked. This leaves us completely vulnerable to the enemy as well as ineffective for God's Kingdom. It has become common to look for things that come without a cost. We need to understand that it cost Jesus His life for us to be a part of His family. He also made it clear that if He had to pay this kind of price, we would have a price to pay as well. Salvation is a free gift, but walking as Jesus walked is another issue.

In the book of Luke, Jesus told His disciples to go and wait in Jerusalem until they were clothed with power from on high. They had to wait more than forty days for God to pour out His Spirit. Why not just a few days? This is an example of the price we pay to receive the promise of God. *Price* is not a very popular term in our society because people have been taught to go straight to the microwave and look for the free deal—everything without price. Many times the grace of God is confused with the price of following God, because people somehow think everything is without cost. Salvation is a free gift. Being conformed into Christlikeness and following in His footsteps has a price tag associated with it. Yet it is God's grace that enables us to pay the price. We see grace and sacrifice work together. Jesus paid the grandest of prices as our primary example.

"Behold, I send the Promise of My Father upon you; but tarry in the city of Jerusalem until you are endued with power from on high" (Luke 24:49). The Holy Spirit came down like tongues of fire upon the 120 people pursuing God. From this time on, they were anointed to go; the heavens were open for them. They were now baptized in the Holy Spirit, being filled and clothed in God's presence. Thanks to Jesus paying the price, we also have an unhindered connection with Him.

Through the singular event at Pentecost, the coming of the Spirit, the heavens are open for our lives. We are not trying to pull God down out of heaven. We do not need to struggle, war and fight to get the heavens open over us. Jesus has already accomplished this through the work of the cross. He busted through the heavens in resurrection glory. The way has been made for each of us to walk in His glory.

What explains the gap between what we know has been accomplished for us through the work of Christ and what we actually experience in our lives? That gap consists of our own personal hunger, devotion and sacrifice. We are the ones who have a responsibility to bridge that gap. If we sit back and do nothing, absolutely nothing will happen. But if we engage our hunger, desire and commitment through sacrificial living, we can then be partakers of His divine nature, bridging the gap of what we know intellectually with the reality of personal experience.

In my own life—as you have perhaps found to be true in yours—I have experienced dryness from time to time. This just serves as motivation to get closer to God. We are learning to live in a place of accessing the waters of His Spirit continually through practicing God's presence daily. Only we can determine our own personal experience. In the beginning

He gave Adam a choice. He always gives us a choice, for He has predestined us to choose. God tells us to choose life or death, blessing or cursing. We have a choice, and He will not take it away from us.

There have been many times when I simply chose to do what I knew to do to experience God's presence, using what has worked in my life. Sometimes it works and sometimes not. But I continue to pursue until I find that breakthrough into His presence. I will search for the key that works for that day. It can be a certain prayer God is looking for, surrender, a song or something else that helps me to break through into an experience with Him. I am always reminded that God will not be put in a box. Things usually do not look the same way twice. He is looking for a pure worship from the heart that cannot be formulized, and He draws near to those who draw near to Him.

Breakthrough Within

The breakthrough we all need is in our own hearts and lives. God wants to awaken us to the treasure of His Spirit that He has already deposited within us. Just as Jesus used the picture of springs of living water flowing out from within us, so a natural spring comes from the depths of the earth. Out of us—earthen vessels, as the Bible describes us—comes this living water of His presence. Scripture also prophesies that we will draw water from the wells of salvation. God Himself, who has come in the form of the Holy Spirit, is Christ in us, the hope of glory, God dwelling inside of us in the Person of the Spirit: "To them God willed to make known what are the riches of the glory of this mystery among the Gentiles: which is Christ in you, the hope of glory" (Colossians 1:27). The heavens need not be opened within us, because the ruler of heaven dwells inside of us. He works inwardly, from the inside out.

"But we have this treasure in earthen vessels, that the excellence of the power may be of God and not of us" (2 Corinthians 4:7). By accessing His life, the treasure of eternity within us, we find our breakthrough also within us, a communion that is far more satisfying than anything on this planet. The enemy attempts to stop up the wells of our lives to keep us ignorant of the good deposit that God has given to us. There is a story from the time of Isaac that paints the picture rather clearly of what the enemy does to hinder God's promise and blessing for our lives:

> And Isaac dug again the wells of water which they had dug in the days of Abraham his father, for the Philistines had stopped them up after the death of Abraham. He called them by the names which his father had called them.
>
> Genesis 26:18

The Philistines had clogged the wells that rightfully belonged to Isaac, so that Isaac had to reopen the wells to enjoy what was there. Why in the world would you clog a well? Only the devil would do something like this. Do you feel as if your well has been clogged? The enemy wants you to be ignorant of what is rightfully yours. Even if you know it is yours, he will do what he can to keep you from experiencing the reality of this provision.

Many times the wells in our lives need reopening so that we can experience the presence of God. How do we open up these wells? Christ in you is the hope of glory. This is not something you are trying to pull out of heaven; it is the substance of His Spirit's presence within you. God will come to help you open up that well in your life as you draw near to Him.

Soaking in the Presence of God

One of the ways we can enter into the reality of Christ within us is through soaking in God's presence. The idea of "soaking" in the presence of God may be new to you. Essentially it means to set your heart to receive in God's presence. David, who was a master at this, is our biblical guide to a lifestyle of connecting with God in this way.

Living Psalm 23

I have heard it said that King David was a New Testament person in an Old Testament era. David knew the satisfaction of God's presence. When he wrote one of the most treasured and beautiful chapters in the Bible, Psalm 23, he was speaking of a place of abiding in the Lord that is so restful, so peaceful and so intimate that it is beyond anything this world can offer. When we discover the still waters of His presence, nothing else can satisfy. Through his life experience, David learned some helpful keys to entering this place, which he recorded in Psalm 23: "The LORD is my shepherd; I shall not want. He makes me to lie down in green pastures; He leads me beside the still waters. He restores my soul" (vv. 1–3).

The first thing David shows us in this psalm is his utter contentment with the Lord as his shepherd. In the first line, he says, "I shall not want." This reveals David's soul's pleasure in God: There is nothing more satisfying than just being with Him. Knowing that the presence of God is with you, that you are in His care, takes care of all other issues.

As we look even more closely, we see the goodness of God revealed when the Good Shepherd "makes" David lie down in the green pastures, which are the best of the best of places. Then He leads him beside the still waters. Imagine the tranquility and solace of the scene, creating a healing environment for the soul. Such is the place of intimacy with God. In God's presence we find a contentment that cannot be found anywhere else. That which seems enormous suddenly becomes small and insignificant. Sometimes people think that if an amazing, substantial event transpired in their lives, they would find contentment. The truth is that the steady progression in our communion with God is what leads us to that rest, refreshing and peace, bringing solace to our souls.

Learning to Release

Soaking in the presence of God means putting ourselves in a physical, emotional and heart disposition in which we release everything to God, laying it all before the feet of Jesus. The anxious pace of this world pulls people away from the things that really matter and have the most eternal value.

"Be anxious for nothing, but in everything by prayer and supplication, with thanksgiving, let your requests be made known to God" (Philippians 4:6). Anxiousness is a thief. It steals your heart from God. It is rooted in fear, for it is just the opposite of love. God wants our hearts so filled with His love that nothing else in this world matters. When fear takes over the helm of a life, then the person will resort to control to make things right; yet he or she will only find frustration and reap superficial results.

The more we try to control, the less we have control. It is like telling your child, "Stop, or else!" It just makes them want to do it more. The only way you can change things is by exemplifying the correct behavior to them. An eye for an eye will make things worse. This is why it is so important to release your concerns, let go and trust the Lord through a life of prayer and devotion. In doing this you are coming out of alignment with darkness and coming into agreement with God.

Countless times in my own life I have been tempted to control a situation. Whenever we are confronted with something that we know needs to be legitimately fixed, we also need to realize that, though we may play a part in seeing it happen, ultimately God is the one who brings the resolution. We should pick our battles wisely. Some things will heal just by resting it out. What do I mean by that? Take a break, give some space and allow God to work in your heart as you pray through the situation. Prayer puts things in God's hands, whereas our intervention will many times cut His off. Then we end up making things worse than before. God is mighty to save, not us.

God's Escape Plan

"They are abundantly satisfied with the fullness of Your house, and You give them drink from the river of Your pleasures" (Psalm 36:8). God has a place for us to run, to enjoy the "fatness" of His house (as it says in the King James Version), the glory of His presence, where we drink from the river of His delights. You may say, "That is escapism!" Yes, it is! God knows that we need to escape. Every person tries to escape from the cares of this world one way or another. People run from the One who is the ultimate escape—Jesus. Jesus really does want us in this world, but He also wants us to know even more the reality of His world. People go on vacations to escape; they go to movies and find all kinds of ways to get away from it all. God provides an escape that is good for us. When we encounter Him in His presence, it is the best possible thing that we could experience. The Bible says that we are changed and transformed by the glory of His face. Jesus said that we would have trials in this life, but to take heart. He has provided a way for us to connect with Him so that we can overcome as well.

Fatness of Spirit

God has designed us to be a people fat in spirit who love the glory of His presence, the dwelling place of His sanctuary. Since that is the case, how do we further fatten our spirits in God? Jesus gave the answer in Matthew 13:23: "But he who received seed on the good ground is he who hears the word and understands it, who indeed bears fruit and produces: some a hundredfold, some sixty, some thirty." There are many seeds we can sow to develop the spirit man to grow in size and effect. God's Word is the "seed" that Jesus refers to as being essential to our lives and the health of our spirit. On top of that, worship and prayer are core elements that cause us to grow.

The catch is when these things become more of a heavy thing rather than something we joyfully engage in. Our devotion should be a joyful engagement, for it is the Father's joy to spend time with us. There is a crossroads where a choice to yield to God intersects the joy of worship and prayer. This is where we start to enjoy being with Him, realizing how much He enjoys us. Try to remove the boundaries of time, whether short or long; just take time to be with Him. Let your spirit grow organically before the Lord. As you do, your spirit will begin to fatten up with the oil of joy.

Receiving His Thoughts

Soaking is not mindless. On the contrary, when we soak in God's presence, we lay down our thoughts and receive His thoughts. As we lie in His presence, we are asking Him to speak to us through His Holy Spirit. This is not a time of Bible study. This is a time when God pulls from the library of our hearts what He desires us to focus on. It is part of allowing God to lead us by His Spirit. God wants us not only to know *about* Him but, more importantly, to *know* Him.

Practical Steps

So, *how* do we tap into the reality of the Holy Spirit? How do we "soak"—practically speaking? For those of you who do not have much practice in this area, there are certain tools that can help you, on a daily basis, quiet your mind, cultivate an awareness of God's presence and foster an ongoing connection with the Holy Spirit.

Key #1: Become Quiet

If at all possible, find a quiet place to rest. Lie down. Get in a physical position that is comfortable. Put on some soaking music to help you feel rested. If you fall asleep, it is okay. In this process you are learning to absorb God's presence, whether you are asleep or awake.

Sometimes you just need a good rest. It is one thing to have quiet in the natural and another thing to have peace and quiet in your heart. Quiet in your heart is what we are after. Sometimes we try to get in a resting place and "the list" pops up. Keep a pen and pad of paper handy; if you need to write things down so you will not forget them in order to get them out of your immediate thoughts, do this. Then set them aside so you can focus your thoughts on the Lord.

Key #2: Focus on Scripture

Use the Word of God to renew your mind and help you focus. You probably will not want the book of Chronicles for inspiration. Get a feel for what is Holy Spirit–directed and inspirational. Genesis 10:24 ("Arphaxad begot Salah, and Salah begot Eber"), for example, might not work for you. Try something like Colossians 3:1–2, about setting your thoughts on things above, which has a much more inspirational flow to it: "If then you have been raised with Christ, seek the things that are above, where Christ is, seated at the right hand of God. Set your minds on things that are above, not on things that are on earth" (ESV). This typically works much better.

Philippians 4:8 has been a favorite verse of mine for my entire walk with God. This is a good place to start. Find a verse that grabs your interest and meditate on it in your devotional time. We have great promises of blessing as we meditate on God's Word. When we meditate, we absorb His truth like a sponge. We are not in a rush. We must learn how to slow down, enjoying our time with God.

> But his delight is in the law of the LORD, and in His law he meditates day and night. He shall be like a tree planted by the rivers of water, that brings forth its fruit in its season, whose leaf also shall not wither; and whatever he does shall prosper.
>
> Psalm 1:2–3

To meditate on something simply means to ponder and chew on it, dwelling on it. This is how we set our thoughts. We all meditate whether we know it or not. In meditation we engage our thinking. We just need to meditate on the things of God, what is pleasing to Him and the truth of His Word.

Key #3: Listen to Soaking Music

Worshipful instrumental music is very useful for helping you get to a place of experiencing God's presence. The reason I say instrumental music is because it is like a clean tapestry every time you turn it on. Worship music is great for worshiping, and there will always be times we need to engage with God this way, giving our worship to Him. But soaking is completely different; it is about receiving from the Lord. For many people receiving is harder than giving. Words can also be distracting at times and overly repetitive.

The best analogy is that instrumental music is like a clear whiteboard you can write on, while music with words is a board that is already scribbled on. In other words, if you use worship music, the words will guide you in the same direction each time. With instrumental music you are free to go any direction the

Holy Spirit leads. This can be used as a backdrop for meditation in the Word or praying in the Holy Spirit, or it can help get you to a place where you can rest in quietness of heart. Sometimes it is effective to start with soaking music, and once you are in a good place of rest, just lower the volume for a quieter experience.

Faith or Feelings

Do not be hard on yourself if you are not experiencing God's presence at the beginning of your pursuit. God rewards faithfulness, not performance. I can tell you of times when I did not feel a thing as I lay in expectation. What I learned to do was to be faithful in that place, whether I felt Him or not. I pursued Him. Then I found Him. He found me. I could be reading the Word with some soaking music playing, on the floor with my legs kicked up on an ottoman, praying in the Spirit, reading a book or just lying in silence. The next thing I knew, I was experiencing the weightiness of His glory on the floor. God uses all these things to bring us into the place of knowing His presence. We do not worship Him by feelings but by faith. All the same, God loves to invade our feelings with His Spirit, sharing His heart with us. David said in Psalm 84:2, "My heart and my flesh cry out . . ."

Reward in the Secret Place

"But you, when you pray, go into your room, and when you have shut your door, pray to your Father who is in the secret place; and your Father who sees in secret will reward you openly" (Matthew 6:6). What God sees in secret will be openly rewarded. Soaking in God's presence is a way to let the Father know how much you appreciate Him. We do not want to take Him for granted or treat Him like a common thing. Know that the time you are spending on the floor, when you could be busy doing other things, will be well rewarded.

Some people have a really hard time slowing down. That can be because of anxiousness and equating activity with productivity. When Mary sat at the feet of Jesus, hearing His words, in the eyes of Jesus this was the most productive thing that she could possibly do. He said that this "one thing" she was doing would not be taken away from her. Just think of all the busyness that people engage in without God. Much of this will go up in flames because God was not the initiator, nor was He involved with or invited into the process. Establish your connection with God early so that you experience His presence even while you engage in other things through the day.

Maybe you are saying, "You have no idea how many things I have to do! The kids, the list, the relatives, the groceries, school . . ." Do what you can. Find a small block of time, even five minutes. You do not have to be on the floor, either. It is not about the position of your body. Sometimes you just have to make a connection with God where you are. We all can find five or more minutes in the day to slow down, rest in His presence and make Him our sole focus. Make the effort. You can do it! Your life depends on it. This is just the start of living before God with your whole heart.

Life Application

- **KNOW** that Jesus opened up the heavens for you personally. Even greater than that, God lives *inside* of you. Tap into "Christ in you, the hope of glory" (Colossians 1:27). You will experience breakthroughs beyond what you can imagine.

- **WORSHIP** God. Close your eyes, lift your hands, lift your voice and make Him your sole focus. As you exalt Him, He will exalt you, giving you the revelation that one day in His courts really is better than a thousand elsewhere!

- **REST** in His presence. Take some time to put on peaceful soaking music without words, or just sit in silence. Lie down on the floor or some place comfortable, in a way you can receive from God. Let go of all thoughts as best you can. Write them down if needed to quiet your soul.

- **EXPECT** God to reward you. When you are faithful with little, He will give you much. Know that your devotion to Him is not in vain. He will draw near to you as you draw near to Him.

4

Wholehearted Living

Blessed are those who keep His testimonies, who
seek Him with the whole heart!

Psalm 119:2

Living for God with your whole heart is more easily understood than practiced. As we are learning to experience
God's presence on a continual basis, we need to grow in living
from the heart rather than leaning on the strength of our natural minds. It is easy to say or sing, "I surrender all," but really
seeing that worked out in our lives is a different story. How
many times do we sing about surrendering but in actuality live
with reservations? Truly living is truly giving our all. For us to
really live, we have to truly give everything that we are to God.
Each of our lives is a seed that can be sown for the Kingdom of
God, for His greater purposes and plans. Our lives are valuable
to God, and He will use us when we make ourselves available.

In my own life I have wrestled with God plenty of times,
just as we all wrestle with God for His blessing and promise

of fulfillment. I remember one season of wrestling with God for His best in my life; it seemed to take a very long time to get through that season into the place of fulfillment. A dear friend of mine who has passed on to be with the Lord, Bob Jones, said, "Good is the enemy of the best." It is called a "good fight of faith" because there is an actual fight. If you stop fighting for what God has promised for you, then you have already lost. Quitters automatically default into defeat.

When Jacob wrestled with God all night long, he knew that Esau was after him. The events of his past were coming to revisit him. It was time for Jacob to learn the lesson, face his fears and move into a greater grace and favor with God. God's grace works with us to get us in position to be vessels He can use. He is not looking for perfection but rather for those who more often imperfectly say yes to His desires.

Back in the '90s I was caught in a place of wanting, not feeling that I was doing all God had called me to. At the time, I was a single man doing anything to make life more interesting. I came to a point when I did not care what it would cost to get to a new place. Out of desperation, I pressed into another level in my walk with God; the better thing that God had for my life became more valuable to me than the pleasures of my current situation. I had to press in, fight and refuse to settle for less than what God had in store. There comes a time when we have to believe that God has a better place for us; we also need the follow-through to pay the price to get there. Out of a hunger for more, a wholehearted commitment emerges, giving birth to dreams, new hope and promise.

Sowing Seeds of Life

We reap what we sow. If we spend our days sowing things of God in our lives, we will reap life and blessing. If we spend our time sowing things of the flesh, our natural appetites and desires, we will reap corruption and destruction. We have to find ways to sow generously to the Spirit so that we may continually reap life. This is basic and yet often easily missed. We need resolve to give ourselves to eternal things, rather than things that are temporary and destined to pass away. How can we get this kind of resolve? It begins by recognizing that our current state is inferior to God's best for our lives.

"So Samuel grew, and the LORD was with him and let none of his words fall to the ground" (1 Samuel 3:19). Samuel was wise in how he invested his life. We can see that even as a child, he was already sowing into eternity through his life of worship before the Lord. This began even before his birth, when his mother, Hannah, dedicated him to the Lord. At the beginning of his life he spent time just worshiping the Lord. Because of the way Samuel's life was invested, God gave him the ultimate protection plan: He would not allow Samuel's words to be wasted. God blesses us when we have an unusual, wholehearted devotion to Him.

Think about how you spend your time during the day. What are you doing? Where is your time going? What are you sowing into? Time is a gift, and we each choose how we are going to use the time we have been given. It is essentially about investment of our time, energy and substance. We need to ask ourselves, "Where should I invest today?"

Lifting the Standard

God likes to raise the bar for us. I recently asked someone about services at his church in Argentina and what it is like to be a part of that church. He said, "Signs, healings, wonders and miracles." This is normal for them. The people there accept it because it is nothing unusual. They have a great hunger for

God, and because of this God responds to their cry. Where there are many options in life, God can become just another option. The desperation is lost. It actually takes a greater dedication and focus to walk wholeheartedly toward God when you have an abundance of options. It takes eyes to see our true condition to create desperation for God within us.

> Do not be deceived, God is not mocked; for whatever a man sows, that he will also reap. For he who sows to his flesh will of the flesh reap corruption, but he who sows to the Spirit will of the Spirit reap everlasting life.
>
> Galatians 6:7–8

As we learn to sow to the Spirit, we will reap from the Spirit. When we seek the Lord with all of our hearts, we will find Him. His promises stand for all of us, because He is no respecter of persons. By raising the bar on our surrender, hunger and faith, we can move into greater realization of His promises and become partakers of His divine nature: "By which have been given to us exceedingly great and precious promises, that through these you may be partakers of the divine nature, having escaped the corruption that is in the world through lust" (2 Peter 1:4). The works that Jesus did are part of our inheritance; it is up to us to claim them.

How can you sow to the Spirit for a transformation in your life and heart? It begins with a surrender to the Lord, just as when you first came to Him for salvation. It requires daily surrender to see the reality of your new spiritual DNA—a DNA that has been created after His image. Begin sowing your time in His presence through prayer and worship. Then do some small, subject-based studies of God's Word. I believe this can be one of the most powerful and transforming ways to study the Bible: Pick a subject that you most need help with personally—maybe fear, or you need more grace, or something else. Look up four or five Scriptures that deal with that subject and meditate on them. In this way you begin to incorporate the heart of God into your life through pondering His truth. God promises joy, peace and love for your life. Begin to believe it by devoting your life to His words.

Our communion with the Holy Spirit helps us become acclimated to God's presence. Sensitivity to God helps us stay in tune with what is pleasing to Him. As we slow ourselves down, God will begin to show us our heart motivations for the things we do. Sometimes it is good to ask yourself, "Why did I say that? Was there a benefit for me? Am I trying to look spiritual or important?" Hundreds of reasons for doing the things we do can replace God as our main motivation. What was Jesus' main motivation for all that He said and did? The Father's pleasure. There was no ulterior motive in His heart. We live in a day when people like to cut corners, throw a lot of things in the fine print, cross the line and twist things to their own benefit. As we talk about serving God with our whole heart, these are the kinds of actions we need to question in ourselves—for the pure in heart shall see God.

Removing Compromise

Is it possible to live a life pleasing to God apart from the Holy Spirit? How can we succeed in not compromising to the spirit of this world if we do not have a sensitivity to the Holy Spirit in our lives? One would think this is impossible. We must understand our deep need for His presence in our lives.

Jesus told us the Holy Spirit is to be the source of our power as witnesses (see Acts 1:8). When we deny or resist the Holy Spirit when He comes to bring us power, we open our lives to a great deception, for we look at God through a blurred lens. Many people in the Church (or in circles that focus on the "organized religion" aspect of it) have lost their moral compass and have settled for performance, perversion, self-exaltation and mediocrity. Could this be the fulfillment of what was spoken to Timothy by Paul?

> But know this, that in the last days perilous times will come: For men will be lovers of themselves, lovers of money, boasters, proud, blasphemers, disobedient to parents, unthankful, unholy, unloving, unforgiving, slanderers, without self-control, brutal, despisers of good, traitors, headstrong, haughty, lovers of pleasure rather than lovers of God, *having a form of godliness but denying its power*. And from such people turn away!
>
> 2 Timothy 3:1–5, emphasis added

In reading this passage, you might initially think that Paul was referring to those who are not associated with religion in any sense. To the contrary, he is referring to those who have "a form of godliness." Then he gives this instruction: "And from such people turn away!" This passage is a red flag for those who think that they can claim to know Christ but not have a life that reflects Him. Because of the integration of worldly ways into the mindsets of many who claim to know God, the word *Christian* no longer conveys that someone is a devoted follower of Jesus Christ.

To many modern-day Christians, the Holy Spirit is a foreigner. If God shows up in a gathering, many are liable to think the people in it are strange because of their passionate pursuit, because of their out-of-the-box approaches or simply for not following the common flow of what is popular. Organized religion either is or can easily become a machine, with toxic effects on the simple cultivation of the intimate family environment so essential for believers. It is not wrong to have organization, but true family life must be preserved by rooting congregations in healthy relationships that foster life in Christ.

Organization is not evil; it is a good thing when it is subservient to God's purposes.

The religious leaders in Jesus' day had also compromised with the spirit of the world. For them it was about the organization and protecting their territory. Their motivation was the love of money and position, self-exaltation and the mechanics of religion, and they were willing to take out anyone who got in their way, *even Jesus*. Modern-day Christianity has taken on this religiosity in many ways. No one is exempt from corruption by this leaven; this is why Jesus told His very own disciples to "beware of the leaven of the Pharisees" (Luke 12:1).

Those who believe in having an encounter with God and the Holy Spirit, who seek any kind of demonstration of the Kingdom, still have to have wisdom. The motives of our hearts are completely separate from anointing, gifting and the blessings of God. We need to allow ourselves to be kept in check, through our relationships with God and others, that we may avoid these religious tendencies.

> Not everyone who says to Me, "Lord, Lord," shall enter the kingdom of heaven, but he who does the will of My Father in heaven. Many will say to Me in that day, "Lord, Lord, have we not prophesied in Your name, cast out demons in Your name, and done many wonders in Your name?" And then I will declare to them, "I never knew you; depart from Me, you who practice lawlessness!"
>
> Matthew 7:21–23

This verse has across-the-board application to anyone who finds identity in anything other than knowing Christ. It all comes down to our intimacy with God. Are you spending time with Him to know Him? Intimacy with God is not a one-night stand; it is a life of faithfulness to His presence in pure devotion. Those who dedicate their lives in pure devotion, God will vindicate, justify and stand up for. We are called to be people who know the Holy Spirit and welcome the Holy Spirit, knowing that He is "Christ in us, the hope of glory."

After I had been walking with the Lord for around two years, my family took me to a movie one day. I was twenty. Since being filled with the Holy Spirit, I had stayed away from all movies, but I agreed to go with them because I did not know what the movie was about. I was in the theatre for just five or ten minutes before I had to leave because I could not handle it. I came out weeping over the movie because my spirit was so grieved. My family, who did not walk with the Lord, did not understand—and rightly so. There is no way they could. But my heart was in such a sensitive place to God that I could not stand to watch the kinds of things the world typically engages in.

Such is the case when we fully give the whole heart to the Holy Spirit. He will make us sensitive to the things that grieve His heart. The Holy Spirit is the one we commune with, the very person who makes our intimacy with God living. We must be willing to embrace a relationship with the Holy Spirit to reflect the image of God and become Christlike.

Learning to keep communion with God, loving His presence, loving one another and pouring out to the world are central. If we focus on creating our own kingdoms, we will fail and fall into a religious rut. The religious spirit molds to any culture—it does not matter what kind of church culture it is. If the emphasis ever becomes more on the culture rather than on Christ, there is an open door for religious pride to enter in. We are to conform to the image of Christ, not a culture. It is okay to honor a culture, but we must conform to Christ.

To have eyes that see and ears that hear, we have to be willing to let go of the exaltation of culture, ritualism and traditions of men. Christ alone deserves to be exalted. A culture or expression means nothing without Him.

Walking with Jesus

Daily we live out our decisions to follow Christ. The Bible describes this as "walking" with Him. There are two primary ways we do this: by cultivating a personal life of devotion to Him and by embracing a community of like-minded Christians who will walk with us on the journey.

Devotional Life

Our devotional life is that time we spend with God in intimate communion. Here is where we let our roots grow deep through personal worship to Him, meditating and studying His words and, through all kinds of prayer, seeking the Lord. It is here that we discover God's manifested presence in our lives. We are given stability to walk with God every day, growing in His presence.

"But I am afraid that as the serpent deceived Eve by his cunning, your thoughts will be led astray from a sincere and pure devotion to Christ" (2 Corinthians 11:3 ESV). Intimacy with God is our foundation. If we lose this foundation, we have nothing concrete to stand on. Intimacy is the point at which we find consistency in our lives concerning His faithfulness. It is a great treasure just to know the reality of communion with His Holy Spirit. This was the anchor in the life of Jesus: knowing the Father. Each day He walked in dependency upon the Father, knowing that apart from Him, He could do nothing.

My own devotion consists of a mix of approaches. I tend to believe that different personalities will drift toward certain aspects of devotion. I am very partial to spending time in worship, for example, because it is part of my gift mix. Someone else could be less like an artist but more like a scientist. That person would prefer different aspects of the devotional life, like intense study of the Word. Neither approach is wrong. But realizing where your strength lies also helps you to know other aspects that you need to work on. A person favoring study will need to be intentional about spending time in intimate worship of God, just as the opposite would apply to one who gravitates toward worship.

Another aspect of devotion that I enjoy and that is highly effective is that of writing down what I am hearing in my moments of intimacy with God. Having a pen and pad ready gets you in position to receive what God is saying. Get inspiration for revelation. The term *revelation* can sound kind of "out there" for some people, but it just refers to God turning the light on in your heart so that you may hear what He has to say to you. It is common to come out of a place of worship with impressions of things God is speaking to you.

Community Life

Community is where we grow together as living stones. It is the habitation of God as the local church body. Here we learn to serve one another, help each other grow in the Lord and bless one another through our interactions in God's presence.

> So continuing daily with one accord in the temple, and breaking bread from house to house, they ate their food with gladness and simplicity of heart, praising God and having favor with all the people. And the Lord added to the church daily those who were being saved.
>
> Acts 2:46–47

What a beautiful picture in the book of Acts of God's people having the simplicity of devotion. There is power in our agreement in the presence of God. I would like to say that this is common, but it is not. It is much more common to find a machine of

74

religion than to find the living organism of community within the local church. The Holy Spirit is the person who brings the bond of unity among us.

When the presence of God is in the midst of His people who have love for God and love for one another, Jesus is lifted up. Jesus told us that the world would know that we are His disciples through our love for one another. Our perception and even our definition of church need to be adjusted. God does not need a building to have a church; the church consists of people who gather together in His name.

Jesus said, "Where two or three are gathered together in my name, there am I in the midst of them" (Matthew 18:20 KJV). Big is not necessarily better. Most everyone likes to follow the crowd, but Jesus was not that way. He said a lot of tough things that only helped to eliminate the crowd. He had only twelve disciples. Then one of those betrayed Him. Even small groups can have this happen. It is notable that Jesus did not get rid of Judas but made him keeper of the money bag. It shows just how vulnerable Jesus made Himself.

In intimate community we make ourselves vulnerable, learning to love, and God's presence is poured out in our midst. One of the best things about being in close community with others is that we have the opportunity to really get to know one another, to pray for, help and serve each other. Even more than that, we get to have fun and enjoy our times in God's presence together.

> Behold, how good and how pleasant it is for brethren to dwell together in unity! It is like the precious oil upon the head, running down on the beard, the beard of Aaron, running down on the edge of his garments. It is like the dew of Hermon, descending upon the mountains of Zion; for there the LORD commanded the blessing—life forevermore.
>
> Psalm 133:1–3

Overflow Life

What we have received, we need to give away. This means finding those who are hungry and thirsty but do not know what they are looking for. We go to offer the waters of life, inviting them to taste and see that the Lord is good. These are great opportunities to pray for people that they may experience the Lord's goodness. I would say a vast majority of people have only experienced religious works. God wants to pour His love out in people.

> A woman of Samaria came to draw water. Jesus said to her, "Give Me a drink." For His disciples had gone away into the city to buy food. Then the woman of Samaria said to Him, "How is it that You, being a Jew, ask a drink from me, a Samaritan woman?" For Jews have no dealings with Samaritans. Jesus answered and said to her, "If you knew the gift of God, and who it is who says to you, 'Give Me a drink,' you would have asked Him, and He would have given you living water."
>
> John 4:7–10

Jesus went on to give the woman prophetic insights into her life. He stirred her interest, making her thirsty for the water of life. When she arrived, she was in her own world. Jesus drew her into His world by the insights given to Him about her life through the Spirit. In the same way, we have the ability to spread the influence of God's love and presence to people who have not experienced Him before. Many think that you need to go through classes, training and more to share God's love. What you really need is to experience God's love yourself in such a way that sharing it comes naturally. It is not about how well you can pray or all the things that you say; it is more about how your life overflows with His goodness and love.

What we have to offer is the best that people can get. When we carry His grace, life and goodness, people will be attracted to it like a magnet. This does not mean we have all the answers to every issue in their lives—but Jesus does. Our role is to help them taste of the goodness of God. This will overflow out of our lives as we live with a whole heart.

It does help, however, to understand all the dynamics that impact a life. What factors affect a life, both spiritually and naturally, that might consequently hinder someone from experiencing the presence of God? We will take a look at some practical spheres of life that affect us all in the next chapter.

Life Application

- **CHOOSE** to sow seeds of life. For every seed that you sow, God will give a greater return to your life. Be thoughtful, be generous and watch God's favor follow you. Treat others as you would like to be treated.

- **COMMIT** to the three components of healthy life: Be faithful to your devotional life with God, find a family to build community with and share the life of God with others who do not know Him.

- **BEWARE** of religious leaven. "Beware" in Mark 8:15 is the Greek word *blepo*, meaning to look at, behold, perceive, take heed. It is a strong word, but Jesus used it. Guard the simplicity of devotion that you have in loving God with all of your heart, soul, mind and strength. Avoid condemning judgments and a critical spirit.

- **WALK** in wisdom and discernment. Just because people speak all the correct words does not mean that they live in communion with God. Ask the Holy Spirit to give you eyes that see and ears that hear.

5

Spheres of Life

Ponder the path of your feet, and let all your ways
be established.

Proverbs 4:26

Some areas in our lives we do not typically classify as "spiritual." Yet all the choices we make can affect our ability to connect with God and experience His presence. God has created us with a spirit, soul and body, and all three areas can help usher us into His presence or keep us from entering into it. I want to address different aspects of these, starting with how we treat our bodies. This is important because sometimes we have to make adjustments in order to maintain a lasting, ongoing, consistent connection with the Lord. How we take care of ourselves does make a difference, in every sphere of our lives, for it affects our sensitivity to God.

Healthy Living

Among the adjustments I personally have had to make was learning how to modify what I eat. Even though I am not your typical ultra-health nut, over the years I have had to adjust and sacrifice to stay in a pretty good place physically. Our bodies change with time; because of this we have to learn how to move with these changes. We make adjustments to what we eat and how we live because our activity levels can plummet as a result of bodily neglect.

When Paul wrote in 1 Timothy 4:8 that physical activity profits little, we need to understand the historical context in which he was writing. In his day everyone walked everywhere, but what was normal then is not so today. On the contrary, our society is geared for visual screens of all kinds and many other things that keep us on our bottoms. If we look back into history, we find a much more natural exercise regime built into people's lives. They lived without cars and machines and all the modern inventions that have so enriched our lives in recent generations. Our blessings can become our curses if we are not wise in how we treat ourselves. This requires us to understand our physical needs.

> Or do you not know that your body is the temple of the Holy Spirit who is in you, whom you have from God, and you are not your own? For you were bought at a price; therefore glorify God in your body and in your spirit, which are God's.
>
> 1 Corinthians 6:19–20

As a disclaimer, I am not talking about extreme fitness. What I am alluding to is our need for general exercise, good eating habits and basic fitness. I will not go into great detail here of what works, because that is an extensive subject. I will just say that it is very important for us to understand that our bodies are temples of the Holy Spirit. If the temple is falling apart, there will be nothing for Him to dwell in.

Our sensitivity to the Spirit can be hindered by bad health. Poor health is a huge obstacle that can hinder our "experiencing"

God's presence. Please take this into consideration if you are having difficulty connecting with God.

God is a healer, but that does not mean we do not also need to use wisdom to live in a higher place of health. When I was twenty, I could go to my college's cafeteria buffet and truly "buffet my body." I could eat just about anything without gaining weight. Part of it was that I had a built-in daily exercise program because I had to walk everywhere on campus just to get to my classes. But as the years passed without any exercise, they began to show in my body. As life goes on, the body's metabolism changes, as does the way it reacts to different foods.

When I was about thirty years old, I discovered I was gaining weight at a much more rapid pace than I had ten years earlier. The worst part of it was that I was mostly ignorant of it; I thought everything was fine, that there was no real issue. I was in denial, but everyone else could tell. I was blind to it. When my eyes were finally opened to the fact that I needed to do something about my weight, I began trying different fad diets. Do you remember the "fat-free" movement? Companies began to package everything with green labels proclaiming the food was "fat-free." I would get anything with the green "fat-free" label—fat-free Fig Newtons, fat-free Twinkies, fat-free chocolate cookies—only to realize I was still getting strangely bigger rather than getting smaller.

It took me some time to get free of addictive foods, and even to realize which kinds of foods caused problems. Not enough can be said for just eating your fruits and vegetables. One of God's first creations was a garden. Hello! This should give us a clue: "I have given every green herb for food" (Genesis 1:30)!

Many of the foods made available to us today have caused tons of health problems for people. All the chemicals, modifications to natural foods and high-sodium content have drastically affected people. Take time to be informed on what goes into food these days. Ignorance is not bliss. It may come back to bite you later in life!

Most canned foods are laden with sodium (just look at the label)—and very bad–quality sodium. High levels of sodium cause dehydration, which also hinders the regular functions of the body. You should never eat anything, really, that has more than five ingredients, whether prepackaged in a can or box. Take a minute to look at how many ingredients you find on labels for the foods you have in your kitchen cabinets. You cannot even tell what most of the added stuff is. You might figure out that they are chemicals, and that is about it. Stick with ingredients you understand and recognize.

When eating red meat or chicken, organic is best. Some say stick with only chicken and fish. Many of the hormones that are used to grow beef, chicken and fish cause cancer. Organic is more expensive, but you will live longer and possibly eat less. All seafood should be wild caught because of what they feed the farmed fish. Antibiotics, hormones, PCBs, neurotoxins, pesticides and other toxins have all been found in farmed fish.

Dairy has not worked well for me, so I typically stay away from it. In Europe it is illegal to use hormones in milk production, and pasteurization is not required. In America it is illegal *not* to pasteurize it, and producers can use all the hormones they want. If you do consume dairy products, keep the source and production process in mind.

Another food to avoid is soft drinks, because high-fructose corn syrup is like poison. Strangely enough, manufacturers put this in just about every product you can imagine, especially if it is a drink. You really must avoid this, for it can cause all kinds of health issues. Water is the best thing you can possibly drink, as our bodies are composed of 50 to 75 percent water. Drink lots of it—the more you drink water, the better you will feel. Remember that in the Bible living water is a type of the

Holy Spirit. God wants us hydrated both in the natural and in the Holy Spirit.

You may be thinking, *John, you are a purist!* Not at all. But as a standard way of living—as the rule—I stick to this plan. It just requires finding out what kinds of foods do what to your body. I will find occasions, however, to break the rule and not be legalistic about it. My mamma always told me, "Do everything in moderation." And then, jokingly, "Especially moderation!"

The reason I share these things is that if your body is having issues, you will have issues connecting with God. Sickness is oppressive. God wants us free from all oppression; He wants us healed and whole. His desire for our lives is heaven on earth. Notice that the lame man Jesus encountered in Jerusalem was trying to get into the waters to be healed. Jesus met him where he was—a picture of our efforts to be healed and how God meets us in the very place we are seeking healing. When we make an effort to change our situation, doing what we can, God meets us in that place. "God anointed Jesus of Nazareth with the Holy Spirit and with power, who went about doing good and healing all who were oppressed by the devil, for God was with Him" (Acts 10:38).

Have you ever found that when you do not feel good, you lose your motivation and energy to do anything? When my body is in good health, I am much more motivated, even more sensitive to God's presence. The reason for the onslaught against our food, this effort to make our food sources bad, is because the devil knows that if he can keep you consistently in bad health, you will always be trying to fix yourself, rather than being a vessel of healing to others.

Books on the subject of good health are all over the place, making it easy to stay informed. Know what is going into your food and how to take care of your body. Modern-day changes in our food make this especially important.

The Soul Factor

Just as our physical health can impact our sensitivity to God, so other factors can also hinder our experience of God's presence. If you are facing challenges connecting with God, these are things to consider. All things we encounter in life have an effect on our ability to grow in God's presence. If something is hindering us, it is necessary to find out what it is so that we can move on to a better place of sensitivity to His presence—and it is possible to do this: "Therefore we also, since we are surrounded by so great a cloud of witnesses, let us lay aside every weight, and the sin which so easily ensnares us, and let us run with endurance the race that is set before us" (Hebrews 12:1).

Letting Go, Moving On

Every one of us has a different history. We grew up with different parents, different friends and different cultures, all of which can shape the way we interact with God. What we accept as normal might possibly be a lie.

We cannot even begin to scratch the surface of all the factors that shape our unique histories. We all have a different story. The important thing is that none of the things of our past are excuses to live inferior lives in the present. Rather, we ask God to wash us and cleanse us so that we can move on into bright futures with a hope.

"To the praise of the glory of His grace, by which He made us accepted in the Beloved" (Ephesians 1:6). Of the challenges the past can bring to the present, rejection is a big one, and many encounter it. Even if you have had abusive parents, all I can tell you is that God is able to cleanse you of your history and give you a fresh start.

We really do not know what other people have gone through. We see the symptoms that are the fruit of what people have gone through in their lives, but that is an outer shell. We cannot compare apples to apples here. I have not gone through what many have had to deal with, and others have not dealt with what I have had to deal with. Everyone gets his or her share of challenges. But some get more than others.

This is why we look to God, who holds the ultimate view, with the perfect vantage point to see into every person's life. He knows each of us inside out. Keep this in mind when you notice someone struggling or someone's imperfections seem all too clear. You never know what they have been through, but God sees our history from beginning to end. We need to lay hold of His grace for ourselves and for others. God wants to help every one of us to move forward.

> Brethren, I do not count myself to have apprehended; but one thing I do, forgetting those things which are behind and reaching forward to those things which are ahead, I press toward the goal for the prize of the upward call of God in Christ Jesus.
>
> Philippians 3:13–14

One of the biggest things we can learn to do in our lives is let go. We have to learn to move on from the past, asking God to give us forward focus. Sometimes part of letting go is leaving things behind. We do not want to get caught up in environments that are not conducive to healing, freedom or a new start in life.

You have got to want a fresh start so badly that you are brave enough to move on to something completely new and different. We need to be willing to step out of the boat, that which is familiar and feels safe, in order to meet Jesus on the water.

At one point in my life I needed a new surrounding, a new place. I had lived in a familiar place for fifteen years, and I sensed that God wanted to take me somewhere new to release new beginnings. There are times when we have to let go of the old and be willing to start afresh in a new landscape. Many times this involves forgiveness—releasing others and choosing not to feel obligated to stay in a place that holds you back from God's best for your life.

God makes sure that each of us gets the opportunity to love, shown through our willingness to forgive and give grace to others. My life has been no exception; I have had my share of times to release and forgive others. Jesus said we are to forgive seventy times seven—seven is the number of completeness. We must completely forgive, releasing people from our hearts. This is more for our own personal freedom than for others'. God's love is never ending; where our love ends, His love begins.

Having Uncompromising Belief

Many are raised in religious environments that teach them what is wrong and what is right. Some of these things can be good and others bad. For many, though, the problem has been that they have not learned or been taught how to interact with God in the Person of the Holy Spirit. Ultimately, the Holy Spirit is the one who teaches all things. Man is only able to do so much.

In my early life I had people to give me a jump start in my faith. But I had to learn to walk with Him on my own, finding out what is really important and what is not. I have learned that there is nothing more valuable in our walk with God than to have the dynamic of the Holy Spirit in our lives. He is the Teacher, the Helper, the Comforter and Guide, and He is essential for us to live in God's presence.

And I will pray the Father, and He will give you another Helper, that He may abide with you forever—the Spirit of truth, whom the world cannot receive, because it neither sees Him nor knows Him; but you know Him, for He dwells with you and will be in you.

John 14:16–17

Along with the Spirit, the Word of God is essential. If a promise is in the Book, we need to believe it. People often make a distinction between the *logos* and *rhema* words of God, which are meant to work together: The *logos* is the written Word of God and is intended for everyone. *Rhema* consists of the words God speaks to us that have personal application and specifics concerning individuals. The Spirit can also give you a *rhema* word from the *logos*. However it works, we must have the personal voice of God in our lives. His personal directions to us are vital for us to grow in His presence. We need both the Scriptures and His words spoken personally to us as we engage in our relationship with Him. As the Holy Spirit opens our spiritual eyes to understand the Word of God, He also gives us personal direction for our lives.

Being an Original

"But now indeed there are many members, yet one body. And the eye cannot say to the hand, 'I have no need of you'; nor again the head to the feet, 'I have no need of you'" (1 Corinthians 12:20–21). In the Body of Christ we need to appreciate our unique differences. People have been built differently by God to serve in different functions. Some are designed to be the life of the party, others are meant to be visionaries, others are to be helpers and still others are able to see the details and intricacies. While one may be extremely creative in a broad visionary way, another can see the tiny details. With all our differences, we are designed to connect in God's presence.

It is important for us to understand others' roles in the Body. When we do, we will more easily appreciate each other, not trying to fit people into our molds. Do not expect people to be like you, but rather encourage people to follow Christ through your example.

For years I was in a time of discovering who I was, finding out how God wanted to use my life and knowing my true identity. The first thing I learned was that I did not want to be a cookie-cutout of anyone else. I was convinced that God intended for me to be the peculiar person He had made me to be, so I set out in that direction. One way I worked that out in my life was in my music.

When I began creating and writing music, I quit listening to everyone else's. This seemed to help me create a sound of my own that was unique, not conforming to the typical pattern of the time. It opened my spiritual ears to hear God sing over me in a fresh way. I went into my own cave of creativity to discover what was in me, and what came out was my own sound instead of a copy of someone else's.

Finding our own individuality is an important aspect of our spiritual growth. Be who God has created you to be, not what someone projects you should be. What do you enjoy? What sound is in your heart? What vision is in your heart? What things are unique to you alone? God is not against your individuality but rather for it. He did not make you a parrot but a person created in His image and likeness—you are an original. You have your own articulation of His life, and you are the only one who can share it. God has made you to have your own particular powerful expression of His goodness. When David joined the battle with the Philistines, he could not wear Saul's armor. It did not fit. That armor was not created for him. People will try to get you to do things their way, but you have to be yourself.

Complete Surrender

We have been created to worship God with fullness of expression. David understood how to worship the Lord. We could learn a lot from someone who wrote the majority of the Psalms, had his victories in the tens of thousands and was considered a prophet of God (see Acts 2:29–30). The Bible shows us that

David worshiped God with all of his might in a most undignified way: "And I will be even more undignified than this, and will be humble in my own sight" (2 Samuel 6:22). It is pleasing to God for us to worship Him with all that we are and with all that we have.

When we engage our entire being in worship—spirit, soul and body—God is pleased. We are created to worship Him with the entirety of who we are, not just a part. With our spirit we worship. With our mind we worship. With our body we worship God, for all that we are was created for His glory. We can sing, speak, dance and lift our voices, integrating all into a massive worship experience before the Lord. There is no question that before anything else, God wants our hearts. But once He has our hearts, the door is open for us to step into the place of ultimate expression and creativity in His presence.

God is not trying to limit us. He is trying to get us out of the box that religion creates. Everything in the Bible is for us. Jesus did not remove anything. He did not come to take away Scripture that had been written previously but to fulfill it and give us better promises! "Do not think that I came to destroy the Law or the Prophets. I did not come to destroy but to fulfill" (Matthew 5:17).

Jesus says, "More freedom! More life! More glory! More love!" When Jesus came to earth, it was only the beginning of the better things of His Kingdom being manifested in His people. "Nevertheless I tell you the truth. It is to your advantage that I go away; for if I do not go away, the Helper will not come to you; but if I depart, I will send Him to you" (John 16:7).

When we surrender the fullness of our lives (spirit, soul and body) to the Lord, we experience a tremendous breakthrough in our lives. God is after the *complete* surrender. He does not want a part of us, but the whole. Surrender is a simple act, but it is in the simplest things that we find the best foundation and the greatest amount of freedom for our lives. Your freedom will in turn cause others to desire that same life, to experience that same goodness of God.

A Panoramic View

Having a broader view of the historical, family, emotional and health factors that make up people's lives can give us a greater compassion for others. We all have our challenges, but some have had more than others. Some have had difficult lives, whether because of their own choices or not. Then there are those who think that only they have had hard lives and use this as an excuse to stay where they are, looking for a reason to justify their current state of affairs. It can be all too easy to categorize people; but not all have the same situation, and we do not all have the "easy fix."

The good news is that God is able and willing to help each person come into a place of wholeness. The better we understand this, the more He can use us in the process of helping people. God has quick solutions for people. He also has solutions that take us through a process. It is not either-or, but both-and. The key for us is to find out what God's heart is concerning people and how He would use us to be part of the solution. God has given us powerful weapons as well that can help us to overcome personally, experience His presence and help others find greater freedom. We will turn to these next.

Life Application

- **HOW** can you live in better health? If needed, find a way to help your body become a temple more fit for the Holy Spirit.

- **WHAT** things do you need to let go of? Are there any people that need to be forgiven? Anything to leave behind? Do not live in the past, but move into your future.

- **YOUR** part in the Body of Christ is important. Take time to discover how you fit into God's plan. Appreciate others' roles, but realize that yours is equally important. Do not try to be something you are not.

- **FIND** new expression in your worship. Try worshiping the Lord in a fresh way, a way that would be new for you. This will help you step out of something old and into something new.

6

Presence Weapons

> For though we walk in the flesh, we do not war according to the flesh. For the weapons of our warfare are not carnal but mighty in God for pulling down strongholds.
>
> 2 Corinthians 10:3–4

At times we have to fight and contend for promises and for our continual experience in the presence of God. There is no controversy over the fact that when we follow God, no matter where we are in the Lord, battles rage against us both as individuals and corporately to keep us from emerging as powerful representatives of God's Kingdom. All creation groans, waiting for the manifestation of the sons of God. That is a call to us to "arise and shine" with His glory upon our lives as living epistles read by every man. To fight the good fight, we need weapons.

In my walk with God I have had to learn how to take up a number of spiritual weapons. The ones I describe in this chapter are tools that the Lord has provided, but they are only as effective as our foundation of intimacy with God. Intimacy with God is the most powerful weapon that we have against the enemy of our souls. Without a genuine relationship with the Father, we are left fighting battles in our flesh, and the empty shell of spiritual language cannot compensate for that. It is like having a gun with no bullets, a cannon with no cannonball or a launcher without a rocket. The fire of intimacy is the ammunition for these weapons, enabling them to be effective and to hit the right targets.

This chapter will serve as an overview and reminder of the powerful resources God has provided for us to overcome our enemy. All of these weapons are mighty and effective, demolishing the power of the enemy when they are brought together in synergy with a living relationship with God. Some may be used almost all the time, while others may be used in seasons. Many times I have had to bring out of the closet, refurbish and reload some of these weapons. You will also see that some of these cross over into the same territory. They are best used in a life that abides in the presence of God, for these weapons are presence weapons.

The Weapon of the Blood of Jesus

> Therefore, brethren, having boldness to enter the Holiest by the blood of Jesus, by a new and living way which He consecrated for us, through the veil, that is, His flesh, and having a High Priest over the house of God, let us draw near with a true heart in full assurance of faith, having our hearts sprinkled from an evil conscience and our bodies washed with pure water.
>
> Hebrews 10:19–22

The first weapon on our list is the blood of Jesus Christ. Without the blood of Jesus washing us, we cannot even enter into the presence of God. This is why the blood of Jesus is at the top. We come before His presence by His blood alone, not by any works of ours. The blood of Jesus is therefore powerful for us because it gains us access to the source of all help.

In the context of Communion (or the Lord's table, or however you would phrase it), we are to examine ourselves beforehand. Outside of this traditional sense, it is still good for us to examine ourselves as we enter into God's presence, coming clean before Him. In this way we give opportunity for the blood of Christ to wash us from impure motives, attitudes or anything displeasing to God. To wage a good warfare, it is important not to have common ground with the enemy. The blood of Jesus cleanses us from that possibility.

From early on in my journey with God, I would ask Jesus to cleanse me from anything that was not pleasing to Him so that I could have unhindered communion in His presence. Dependence on what He has accomplished is the humble approach we take before His throne. Part of that life of dependence on God includes a heart of surrender in worship.

The Weapon of Praise and Worship

Psalm 100:4 says, "Enter into His gates with thanksgiving, and into His courts with praise." With thanksgiving and praise in our hearts we enter into His presence. To engage with God, our hearts need to be cleansed from all complaint, which is the opposite of thanksgiving. Often we do not think about this. It is not just offering empty words of thanksgiving but truly giving thanks to God from the heart. Gratitude is mere acknowledgment that someone has done something good for you; thanksgiving is expressed when we vocalize that gratitude. God does not call us just to be grateful but to give voice to our gratefulness, because He wants to hear it.

How many times have you heard the phrase, "It's the thought that counts"? Nonsense. It is the follow-through that counts. Jesus taught us that we are not just to think nice thoughts about His commandments; rather, they should be obeyed. "Jesus answered and said to him, 'If anyone loves Me, he will keep My word; and My Father will love him, and We will come to him and make Our home with him'" (John 14:23). We are to vocalize our worship to God. The powerful benefit to that comes when He inhabits our praise. A great matriarch of the faith, Ruth Ward Heflin, wrote this line: "Praise until the spirit of worship comes, worship until His glory comes, then stand in the glory."* God desires our worship to be an experience with Him, not just empty words with no substance or meaning.

The Weapon of His Presence

The presence of God is a most powerful weapon, such that we must have His presence with us. When Moses faced God on behalf of the idolatrous Israelites, God offered to send angels with him to finish the journey to the Promised Land. That was not good enough for Moses. "Then [Moses] said to Him, 'If Your Presence does not go with us, do not bring us up from here'" (Exodus 33:15). Moses declined God's offer of angelic escort, telling God instead that His presence *must* go with them. Without the presence of God in our lives, we will suffer defeat. His presence holds everything together, causing success at every turn.

As we grow in a worship life with God, we are creating a new atmosphere around us, the atmosphere of heaven on earth. As you engage in worship with the Lord, do it with an expectation of His presence coming to fill you, creating an atmosphere

*Ruth Ward Heflin, *Glory: Experiencing the Atmosphere of Heaven* (Hagerstown, Md.: McDougal Publishing, 2016), intro.

around your life. Do not allow your worship experience to be empty but rather filled to overflowing. As you are filled with the waters of His presence, it makes everything in your life much easier.

Jesus walked in the manifested presence of God every day. The only time the presence of God left Him was for a moment on the cross, the moment He cried, "Father! Why have you forsaken me?" He had lost the closeness of God's presence, which He had always experienced. He endured this separation once for all of us. He made a way for us to live now in His presence every day.

The Weapon of the Word of God

"And take the helmet of salvation, and the sword of the Spirit, which is the word of God" (Ephesians 6:17). The Word of God is our main offensive weapon against the enemy. It is a cleansing agent for our souls as well as the truth that we use against the lies of the devil. When Jesus was tempted in the desert, He used the Word of God to confront the devil. Satan actually twisted the Word of God to make it self-gratifying. When Jesus responded with the truth of the Word, He gained victory over the temptations. It is not enough to know the letter of the Word; it must be revelation to us. It needs to be light to our souls. We can read the Word of God, but it needs to "read us" so that our heart motives may be revealed and cleansed. The Word of God, made alive in our hearts by the Holy Spirit, protects us from deception and enables us to walk in His pure truth.

As we meditate on God's Word, we find opportunities to come into agreement with God and to stand on His truth. His Word gives us the blueprint for where we are going. It is the lamp to our feet and the light to our path. It purifies our hearts and renews our minds. God's Word is His will for our lives.

It shows us who we are and where we are going. We should be reading the Word of God daily to get God's heart and sow the good seed in our hearts. The Holy Spirit and the Word work together to cleanse us. Just as a guitar is tuned with a tuning instrument, so the Word of God tunes us to His pitch, bringing us into alignment with His truth. The Word of God is the foundation for our beliefs; therefore, faith comes by our continual meditation on Scripture.

The Weapons of Faith and Love

Without faith it is impossible to please God (see Hebrews 11:6). Our faith is not dependent on our feelings but realized through our actions. Have you ever had a time when you did not "feel" faith for something, but at the same time you knew it was the will of God? Many times we have faith in the lack of feeling faith, or even in the face of fear. At other times, though, we actually do have faith in our hearts for something, maybe even a gift of faith to see it come to pass.

"For we walk by faith, not by sight" (2 Corinthians 5:7). In other words, we do not have to see it, feel it or hear it to believe it. We choose to believe it. As Jesus said to Thomas, this is the higher standard:

> Then He said to Thomas, "Reach your finger here, and look at My hands; and reach your hand here, and put it into My side. Do not be unbelieving, but believing." And Thomas answered and said to Him, "My Lord and my God!" Jesus said to him, "Thomas, because you have seen Me, you have believed. Blessed are those who have not seen and yet have believed."
>
> John 20:27–29

It is the same for those who, even when they do not feel it, still step out onto the waters with Jesus and watch Him do His miracles. Our actions speak louder than what we feel—because, whether we feel it or not, the bottom line is whether we took action on it. Our actions make our faith complete. Faith without actions is dead. God responds to persistence, and faith does not quit. It is better to go for it with all the adventure, excitement and wonder that go along with it than to wait to have all the answers, with everything figured out.

We see this in the life of Peter, who was willing to get out on the water with Jesus, and in blind Bartimaeus, who was willing to look bad in front of others to receive his sight (see Mark 10:46–52). We also see it in the lady who was called a "dog" by Jesus but would not relent in begging for her daughter's healing, saying, "Even the little dogs eat the crumbs which fall from their masters' table" (Matthew 15:27). In all of these examples, we see a willingness to sink, to look bad, even to be insulted—all of which are associated with the life of faith, in which we are not too concerned about our reputation because desperation has taken over.

To live this way, we need a revolution in our faith. A revolution is defined as a turning. God wants to turn our lives in His direction to follow in the footsteps of faith, so that we live dependent on Him in every aspect of our lives. Revolution is also defined as a change in government. God wants to govern our lives to live in His presence with a radical faith, like a bulldog that will not let go of the bone (see Luke 18:1–8). In essence faith is totally focused on the goal without concern for the extreme actions needed to get there. God has given every one of us that measure of faith. This faith resides in us and is ready to be activated in a revolutionary way.

Faith alone, however, is not enough; Galatians 5:6 says, "But faith working through love." There is nothing more powerful than an atmosphere of God's love. Where love exists, an environment is created that facilitates trust, faith, hope and believing.

Faith works through love. This means that where love exists, faith is "energized"—the Greek word for "working" in Galatians 5:6 is *energeo*, which means to be active, fervent and effective.

When we live as conduits of God's love, we are also carrying an atmosphere that will energize and empower faith in the hearts of people. Hatred and bitterness create all kinds of negative fear and distance, whereas love and acceptance create a closeness, intimacy and trust, breeding true faith in the heart.

I went to summer school once during my college years, and I lived in the dorms of my college campus. I did not get to select the person I would share my dorm room with that summer. The person selected for me, I soon discovered, was into New Age, Dungeons and Dragons and reading all kinds of occult books, along with listening to the music that accompanies them. It was a long summer. I knew another guy in the dorm whom I would give rides to when he needed them, so he was around to observe the situation. There came a day that I walked into the dorm room, stood in the middle of it and told the Lord, "Either he is leaving or I am." Literally within a minute, my roommate walked in to tell me that he was leaving. My strong charismatic influence, the Holy Spirit and the things he was into were not compatible. It had been very difficult and spiritually challenging up to that point.

After he left, I thought it was over—but no. It had only begun! Practically every night the rest of that summer, at midnight, my former roommate would sneak over to my room and shoot pop bottle rockets under the door. They would explode and fill the room with a smoky stench. Most every night I would end up leaving the room and walking the campus to pray—it gave me a chance to connect with God and to breathe! That went on through the summer, so I had many of these unscheduled prayer walks.

The next semester the guy who was observing all of this was sent on deployment to fight in Operation Desert Storm under President George H. W. Bush. As I was walking on campus one day, I saw this soldier, dressed in military fatigues, running toward me. He told me that he had just returned. During his time in the Middle East he was baptized in the Holy Spirit and was completely changed. He told me that before he had been deployed, he thought I was completely crazy—I was this strange Spirit-filled, tongues-talking guy. But now, he said, he understood me. God used the way I had treated my ex-roommate the previous summer to touch his life. He saw God's love in action, and it affected him without me even knowing it. I felt the Spirit so strongly in that moment that I began to weep. It was one of those times in life you never forget. Faith works by love.

Where many stumble is in their attempt to walk in faith outside of a love paradigm. Understanding and experiencing the love of God is foundational for faith to be active in our lives and in the lives of others. It makes all the difference.

In our lives we need to make sure we are expressing God's love. Does our behavior create distance or closeness in our relationships? Do we project love in our actions, or are we exemplifying controlling behaviors and tendencies? "And now abide faith, hope, love, these three; but the greatest of these is love" (1 Corinthians 13:13).

The Weapon of Prayer

There are many kinds of prayer, and I will not get into every one. The important thing is that all forms of prayer are effective. My favorite type is praying in the Spirit. That is mainly because it most often connects me with the presence of God quicker than any other method of prayer.

When I speak of "praying in the Spirit," I am referring specifically to speaking in tongues. In the Bible, Paul explains that when we pray this way, we do not understand what we are saying: "For he who speaks in a tongue does not speak to men but to God, for no one understands him; however, in the spirit he speaks mysteries" (1 Corinthians 14:2). Praying with the spirit is a direct connection to God that bypasses the natural mind. The natural mind likes to have everything figured out; it wants to know everything. Praying in tongues is a good practice for the very reason of taking away from your mind the right of "knowing it all." Some things we need to know; others we do not.

The gift of speaking in tongues is available to every believer in Jesus Christ, as Peter testified, "In truth I perceive that God shows no partiality" (Acts 10:34). Ask the Lord to fill you with His Holy Spirit and give evidence of it with the gift of tongues. When we pray with our spirit, we build ourselves up, edifying the spirit man (see 1 Corinthians 14:4).

"What is the conclusion then? I will pray with the spirit, and I will also pray with the understanding. I will sing with the spirit, and I will also sing with the understanding" (1 Corinthians 14:15). Before my conversion experience, I remember trying to read the Bible, the *living* Bible. It made no sense to me and was a very hard read. This was The Living Bible version, about as easy a read as anything you can find—so it should have been easy, even for me! I had been baptized in water but had not learned what living for God looked like. When I was baptized in the Holy Spirit, my understanding of the Bible opened up. As I practiced praying in the Spirit, speaking in tongues in my times with God, His words began to come alive and make sense.

"Put on the new man which was created according to God, in true righteousness and holiness" (Ephesians 4:24). The spirit man is created in the image and likeness of God. When we engage in prayer, we renew the spirit man. There is no quicker or better way to do this than by simply praying in tongues. "[You] have put on the new man who is renewed in knowledge according to the image of Him who created him" (Colossians 3:10).

Paul said that we should pray to interpret what we are saying by the Spirit (1 Corinthians 14:13). When we pray for interpretation, we are basically asking that God would give us revelation and understanding. Many times when I am praying in the Spirit, I will instantly get wisdom and understanding. God may show me something new out of His Word that I would not have otherwise seen. He may also give me direction in things concerning my life. Paul wrote that we pray mysteries with the spirit. When we pray in tongues, the Holy Spirit can use this to pray what He knows needs to be prayed when we do not know. When we use our natural tongue, even though it is valid and needed, it is limited. There is no limit to the span of influence and effect of praying in the Holy Spirit.

Praying in tongues is one way we can stay in a place of consistent communion with the Holy Spirit—it is the heavenly language God has given to us. We can experience the most intimate of relationships with Him through this vehicle of prayer, meanwhile building our faith at an exponential rate. "But you, beloved, building yourselves up on your most holy faith, praying in the Holy Spirit, keep yourselves in the love of God, looking for the mercy of our Lord Jesus Christ unto eternal life" (Jude 20–21).

The Weapon of the Name of Jesus

Have you ever tried to get into God's presence but just could not seem to get there? You are not alone. One weapon I have learned to use in my walk is the outward expression of our pursuit of God. There are many ways to do this, but a very important one is to verbally take authority over the power of the enemy in the name of Jesus.

When things are not clicking, I begin to examine things that may have affected me spiritually—things that can rub off from other sources. All of us engage with different people throughout the day, some of whom have been engaging in things that are not good. While I believe greater is He who is in me than he who is in the world (see 1 John 4:4)—we are the greater influence and should be the dominant factor in our dealings with others—times still come when we have to use the name of Jesus to break off oppression that comes from being around those who carry the wrong atmosphere and are sitting under the wrong influences.

We need to be God-conscious people; I do not believe we should be focused on darkness. But when confronted with it, we need to hit back. We have the power to do this because Jesus gave us authority over all the power of the enemy. We will all confront demons and darkness from time to time. If Jesus did, we will have to also.

Darkness is not hard to find; it is prevalent on television, and as a believer you should be able to see the perversion, violence, anger and other expressions of the kingdom of darkness. Many struggle to be free from darkness, not realizing they are opening the door to demonic influences through media, movies and television. Those who believe in Jesus should ask the Lord for discernment and close the doors through which darkness has filtered into their lives. You cannot expect freedom, abundant life or a life filled with the Holy Spirit if you commune with the wrong kingdom.

> For what fellowship has righteousness with lawlessness? And what communion has light with darkness? And what accord has Christ with Belial? Or what part has a believer with an unbeliever? And what agreement has the temple of God with idols? For you are the temple of the living God.
>
> 2 Corinthians 6:14–16

These things have no place for the believer in Christ. What relationship has light with darkness? You cannot drink of the cup of the Lord and demons. Why do I bring this up? Because of the many people who go to counselors and seek other means of finding freedom but are unwilling to shut the doors of their hearts to demonic influence. Because of this the name of Jesus has no power in their lives. It is God's plan for us to live in freedom, but we have to choose it as well. Jesus came to heal all who are oppressed. Demons oppress people. If you are willing to shut the doors to darkness, then Jesus will happily set you free. Then you will understand the power that is in the name of Jesus! "Therefore God also has highly exalted Him and given Him the name which is above every name" (Philippians 2:9). This is not only for yourself but so that you can be the vehicle God uses to set others free.

Along with the name of Jesus, we can take up another powerful weapon that requires vocal release: high praise.

The Weapon of High Praise

"Stand fast therefore in the liberty by which Christ has made us free, and do not be entangled again with a yoke of bondage" (Galatians 5:1). In the biblical account of Israel's slavery in Egypt, we see that the Israelites were oppressed under a hard yoke of bondage. God does not want us oppressed. If we come under oppression, then we come under that yoke of slavery, and everything becomes difficult. Is that possible for a Christian? Absolutely. But when it is broken off our lives, we are able to take on the easy yoke of Jesus that He has provided for us. It is for freedom that Christ has set us free.

"Let the high praises of God be in their mouth, and a two-edged sword in their hand" (Psalm 149:6). David is a great example of someone who could do this: He was not only a worshiper but a warrior. He understood how to take on different aspects of God's nature at the same time. Worship was his foundation, but becoming a warrior was necessary for him to inherit the nation. As he matured as a warrior, he did not leave the place of true worship; rather he built on that foundation of intimacy with God.

In our worship we must remember that there are times when it is necessary to be a warrior. We need to express ourselves as warriors because it is how God made us; otherwise we regress to expressing anger, bitterness and violence toward people instead of the enemy. We are to fight the good fight of faith in which we believe, contend and move forward in the heat of the battle. People of God's presence are not timid, apathetic or complacent. Rather we are warriors that emerge out of the light of God's presence, ready to take down every opposition that stands against His Kingdom being established in the earth.

Did you know that you are created with "trumpetlike" capabilities?

> The sons of Aaron, the priests, shall blow the trumpets; and these shall be to you as an ordinance forever throughout your generations. When you go to war in your land against the enemy who oppresses you, then you shall sound an alarm with the trumpets, and you will be remembered before the LORD your God, and you will be saved from your enemies.
>
> Numbers 10:8–9

The priests were commanded to blow the trumpets in battle; through this the Lord would grant them victory. There is power in the priestly life, in which we can release our voices like trumpets and see the Lord wipe out our enemies. From deep within our spirits, we can release a sound that breaks the power of darkness. This is how we were created: Our bodies resemble an audio speaker. We have a bass woofer, the belly and chest area, which provides most of the power. We also have a tweeter, our nasal area, which may not have a lot of power, but a little goes a long way when it is needed.

Lifting the high praise is like blowing the trumpet of your being. When our hearts and motives are pure, a glorious release can occur as we lift our voices like trumpets! See your enemy, see your resistance, see the thing that you need to overcome, see the breakthrough that you need—and then begin to lift your voice as a trumpet in praise to God over these things! Add to it another weapon I have found to be most effective in catapulting your spirit to another level: fasting.

The Weapon of Fasting

"Blessed are those who hunger and thirst for righteousness, for they shall be filled" (Matthew 5:6). Have you ever been in a place where things just do not seem to be moving? There may be times when you feel as though you have lost connection with the Lord, and you are having a hard time discovering that intimate place with Him. You can help get things back on track, but it is certain that if you plan to do nothing, nothing is exactly what will happen. Do not allow yourself to drift aimlessly, hoping that something will change. Make good decisions that will lead you on a path of awakening.

The first thing you can do to get yourself tuned in to God's presence is to do "nothing." That is right, you need to do nothing! But you need to do a *particular* nothing, which is, in fact, the absence of something.

The Absence of Something Is Nothing

"I humbled myself with fasting; and my prayer would return to my own heart" (Psalm 35:13). David discovered that when he removed food from his belly, prayer returned to his heart.

Sometimes we just need to reestablish communication. It may not take all that much fasting to bring you into a place of sensitivity to His presence. Sometimes we just get in a pattern of eating just for the sake of eating. Breaking that pattern to focus on the Lord can be just the thing you need to help give you a breakthrough in His presence. It may be one meal or for a day (see Mark 2:20). The key here is that you realize that it is not just the absence of food but the desire to be with God that will cause things to shift. Let your spirit awaken. "The spirit of a man is the lamp of the LORD, searching all the inner depths of his heart" (Proverbs 20:27).

Create Atmosphere

When you skip your meal(s), make sure to incorporate times of worship, vocalizing your love for God. There is nothing more powerful than creating an atmosphere that exemplifies "heaven on earth." Find a room in your house, begin soaking in God's presence and take time to create that heavenly atmosphere. When we welcome the Holy Spirit to fill our homes, He comes and washes us, cleansing all of the spiritual debris away. When we make the Lord our dwelling place, we will create an atmosphere in every aspect of our lives where He is welcome. When He is our dwelling place, He makes His home with us. "Because you have made the LORD, who is my refuge, even the Most High, your dwelling place, no evil shall befall you, nor shall any plague come near your dwelling" (Psalm 91:9–10).

Read, Write and Muse

While you are creating this atmosphere, try to make a comfortable place for yourself. Get your Bible. Remove all your preconceived thoughts. Then ask the Holy Spirit to show you what topic, word, Scripture or book He would have you read and meditate on. Grab your pen and paper and be ready for the Lord to speak to you. Ask God to give you His heart, wisdom, revelation and understanding. Be open to whatever God would show you. It may be something that is completely practical, an inspiring idea or such. Sometimes He will give us things that make us think, *Oh, this is not spiritual*. But in reality it is because He is speaking it to you.

"In the beginning God created the heavens and the earth" (Genesis 1:1). We need to remember that God created all things; He is the most creative person of all. Creative ideas will come when you get in contact with the Creator. Get tapped in to the creative nature of God. Allow His Spirit to inspire you. You will get some things to add to your to-do list; write them down and come back to them after your time with God so that you can rest and focus in His presence. Take time to *receive* what He is wanting to give to you. Unless we receive from Him, we have nothing to give. Do not allow fasting to become a legalistic thing, but let your motivation be to draw close to God. Jesus paid the highest price to bring us back into relationship with Him through the cross. Always keep that in mind—it is not about our sacrifice but His.

The Weapon of the Cross

"Looking unto Jesus, the author and finisher of our faith, who for the joy that was set before Him endured the cross, despising the shame, and has sat down at the right hand of the throne of God" (Hebrews 12:2). When Jesus endured the cross, it was for the joy of many sons and daughters coming into the vast inheritance of His Father. We were His joy. Coming to do the Father's pleasure, He paid the very highest of prices that we might live. He wanted us to know His love, experiencing oneness with Him through His Spirit. Laying down His life on the cross, Jesus became the bridge between God and man. He is the chief intercessor, bridging the gap through love and sacrifice.

Years ago I had an experience at the dentist's office. I had an appointment to get my wisdom teeth removed, and I remember lying on the dental recliner. The oral surgeon asked if I felt anything, and the next thing I knew, I was waking up. He had put me to sleep. I had not known he was going to do that. During the time I was asleep, I had a vision of Jesus on the cross. When I awoke, I was weeping because I had seen Jesus hanging there and all I could think was that He had no painkillers.

Another time I was driving down the road with some worship music on. The song was saying, "Ask what you will . . . ask what you will." I had a vision of Jesus on the cross in which He was saying this. My heart was rent because He had just laid down His life—what more could He give? But He was still saying, "Ask what you will," because He died not only to give us salvation but that we would live in the fullness of what He accomplished through the cross.

"I have been crucified with Christ; it is no longer I who live, but Christ lives in me" (Galatians 2:20). The work of the cross is perfect. All that was needed to pay for the sins of all mankind was covered in the cross. Our lives in Him are secured in the cross, for when He died, we died that we might be alive to God. See your self crucified with Christ. See your self risen with Christ. He gave Himself up for us that we might live in His abundant life today. When we see the finished work of the cross, our confession establishes the reality of what He has accomplished in our lives, causing us to live in a place of wholeness before God.

The Weapon of the Prophetic

Life and death are in the power of the tongue. The words we speak have power and are able to reverse circumstances and create life. He made us with the power to speak, shout and make sounds that release God's light into the atmosphere. When our lives are lived with pure hearts in His presence, there is nothing that can stand against the glory of God manifested through us.

Creative Power

Everything God made in creation is original and diverse in its own way. The beauty in His creation is apparent both in the individual and in the whole. If all the things He made looked the same, it would be a very boring picture. But God knows what He is doing.

He is the author and creator of life, making all things good by the power of His voice. The voice of the Lord brings all things into existence: "God, who gives life to the dead and calls those things which do not exist as though they did" (Romans 4:17). Being created in the image of God, we too have creative power. We hold the ability to transform atmospheres, speak things into existence and cause life to come forth by the power of the Holy Spirit that lives within us. The tongue is one of the most powerful forces that we have in our human makeup.

It is true that "the tongue is a fire, a world of iniquity. The tongue is so set among our members that it defiles the whole body, and sets on fire the course of nature; and it is set on fire by hell" (James 3:6). The human tongue may be a "world of iniquity," but we know that was not the case with Jesus. When Jesus spoke, He was releasing the "world of glory." The glory realm of God was released through Jesus' words, causing life to come forth in every place He spoke. This same power resides in our tongues as well. The tongue is a powerful force the devil has no ability to contradict—just as John testified, when God spoke, light was released and the darkness could not comprehend it (see John 1:1–5). The powers of darkness cannot compete with the "world of glory" that is released through vessels of the

Kingdom of God! He who is in us is much, much greater than he who is in this world. The power of the glory of God wipes out resistance and leaves the enemy whimpering on the floor.

Clean Vessels

Because our words are powerful, we need to realize how important it is to keep our hearts pure. If we speak foolishness and gossip about others, we are empowering the wrong kingdom. Divisiveness is never the heart of God. We need to do all we can to preserve unity with each other through honor. We need not agree, but we do need to be respectful. If anyone has been caught in this trespass, the cure is to *be quick to repent*. Repentance is more powerful than apology. We can say we are sorry all day long; it is better to just change direction. Jesus is continually interceding for His people, and our role is to join Him in the most powerful place of influence. "Therefore He is also able to save to the uttermost those who come to God through Him, since He always lives to make intercession for them" (Hebrews 7:25).

The Priestly Life

HOLY TO THE LORD is our heart consecration to God. It is this dedication, commitment and integrity that will cause the substance of His power to be released in us and through us.

The grace of God has qualified us to live lives of true worship. Having pure hands and clean hearts enables us to carry His glory for the long haul. God calls us higher and deeper into His presence. As plantings of the Lord, we want our roots to go deep into the soil. It is possible to have amazing experiences and yet have shallow roots. External activity does not necessarily equate to internal devotion. To have fruit that remains, we will need to dig a little deeper. Integrity, purity and selfless devotion

112

are foundational for a sincere life of worship. Jesus lived the ultimate example of a life without fault in pure devotion to the Father. He lived for the pleasure of obeying the Father, not out of legalism but out of a living love for the relationship.

The Weapon of Obedience

The simplicity of obeying God will cause His blessings to come upon our lives. Instead of trying to do as many things as possible to please God, we should ask ourselves, "What is the one thing He is telling me to do right now?" It is all too easy to waste our time getting caught up in too much activity. Those who wait upon the Lord shall renew their strength, mounting up with wings as eagles (see Isaiah 40:31). That means we need to wait on Him, hear His voice and serve His purposes. A small amount of obedience to God will always outweigh a multitude of sacrifices.

Our weapons are powerful and helpful for us in walking out His plans for our lives. Some of the ones I have taught about are not necessarily presented as "weapons" in Scripture; their use as weapons is found between the lines. Even so, all of these truths have a far-reaching impact for our lives as we embrace them. God also wants us to be a people of encounter who know the reality of the realm of heaven. In the next chapter, we will look at the awe-inspiring domain of God's throne.

Life Application

- **PRAY** in the Spirit, speaking in tongues. God has provided this as a direct path into His presence. If you have not found release in this yet, pursue the Lord for this gift. It is okay to eagerly desire spiritual gifts (see 1 Corinthians 14:1). Find others you can trust to help if you need it.

- **WELCOME** the spirit of revelation. Allow God to open the eyes of your heart. Ask Him to show you what He would have you see. Ask before going to sleep that He may speak to you in a dream.

- **TAKE** authority when needed. The name of Jesus is the name above every name. Every devil has to bow its head to that name. Whether it be sickness, anger or any other oppression, it must bow to the name of Jesus.

- **STAND** in your liberty. Allow the powerful light of God's presence to fill you, keeping you free from all oppression.

7

The Throne of His Glory

> Immediately I was in the Spirit; and behold, a throne
> set in heaven, and One sat on the throne. And He
> who sat there was like a jasper and a sardius stone
> in appearance; and there was a rainbow around the
> throne, in appearance like an emerald.
>
> Revelation 4:2–3

The space around the throne of God is a place of dramatic encounters. A river proceeds from the throne, which is surrounded by a rainbow, and lightning, thunder and voices issue forth. Angels gather around—living creatures full of eyes on the inside and out; elders clothed in white robes with crowns of gold; seven burning lamps of fire. With these gather the saints, as the four living creatures constantly say, "Holy, holy, holy, Lord God Almighty, who was and is and is to come!" (Revelation 4:8).

The sounds of heaven, thanksgiving and worship are happening nonstop around the throne of God. This gives you an idea of what we experience when we have a throne room encounter with God. The location of God's throne is the third heaven, of which Paul writes of having visited: "I know a man in Christ who fourteen years ago—whether in the body I do not know, or whether out of the body I do not know, God knows—such a one was caught up to the third heaven" (2 Corinthians 12:2).

What Paul saw was beyond words. He was caught up in heaven in something like Eden—like paradise. Such is the setting of the throne of God: It is the center of heavenly worship, activity and amazement. Paul was blown away by this experience. He did not know what to do with this encounter because it was a shock to his system. Seeing these glimpses of God's world is the kind of experience that changes our lives. As we draw near to God, He takes opportunities like this to make His world that much more real to us.

The throne of God is one of my favorite subjects of all because it reminds me of the glory of heaven, the centrality of Jesus and the Lamb upon the throne, combined with all of the amazing sights of worship in heaven. Worship is heaven's very atmosphere. God invites us into this most glorious atmosphere to take part in this gathering of eternity. When we engage in worship, we are actually joining a great company of worshipers on earth and in heaven, pulling the weight of His presence onto our lives.

At our church we hold meetings called "Presence Nights" regularly, where the main emphasis is our corporate engagement in worship and prayer. I can remember one time when we hit a chord in our worship together and the manifested presence of God came in such a way that a fragrance filled the room. At first I thought the scent came from someone walking by who had overused perfume. But it was the smell of burning incense. I stopped to ask others if they could smell this, and many people in the room lifted their hands. Then I realized this was the fragrance of heaven mingled in the worship and prayers of

His people. God inhabits the praises of His people (see Psalm 22:3), and in this case it was in the form of burning incense. This is just one example of what can happen, how heaven and earth interact when we come together as one in our worship.

The book of Revelation is an amazing account of John's vision of Jesus Christ. Jesus is exalted to the highest place in John's encounter. Jesus is the Lamb seated on the throne, the soon-coming King with a two-edged sword coming from His mouth. This is imagery much like what we see in the book of Ezekiel, with the four living creatures in the likeness of both men and animals, and wheels full of eyes.

What a wild book. I can remember my grandpa saying that John must have been on something because the book's imagery is so fantastic. John was actually on Some*one*, the Holy Spirit. But Grandpa was right in that there are some really far-out images in Revelation. Just imagine seeing the living creatures that are "full of eyes" on the inside and the outside (see Revelation 4:8)!

This is one part of the amazing, mind-blowing wonder of God's world, a world He has opened up for us to dwell in. God wants His heavenly world to become real to us. Communing in the presence of God, beholding His glory, helps us to experience the wonder of His world. God lives in a realm far different from earth. We are a peculiar people created to live in the very extraordinary realm of heaven. In all the eye-opening events and judgments that take place in Revelation, its number one message is that Jesus is the center of all things, and everything revolves around Him.

"Come Up Here"

A throne represents authority or the one who is in power. There are "thrones" of spiritual darkness set up geographically throughout the earth. But God wants His throne established

117

throughout the world, displacing the darkness. When Jesus came, He told us to pray the Kingdom and will of God in the earth, that His authority and dominion may be established. He was essentially telling us to establish His throne on earth.

Wherever we are, we are to be establishing His throne. This is not a person's throne, his ministry or her own personal agenda. This is heaven on earth, where God's glory is changing atmospheres and the hearts of men. When His throne is established, heaven invades earth, His power is demonstrated and lives are changed.

Worship has many expressions. It is in essence anything we do to glorify God with our lives. *Throne room worship* is a term used to describe one of the most intimate expressions of worship, in which we are literally entering into the throne room of heaven and worshiping at the feet of Jesus through our vocalization of worship and praise.

With the humanism in the world, the "works orientation" and the pride of life in man's accomplishments, it is important not to overlook the purpose of our vocalizing our worship to God. God is the only one worthy of glory. David praised God among the peoples: "I will praise You, O LORD, among the peoples, and I will sing praises to You among the nations" (Psalm 108:3). If we have a hard time vocalizing our worship in front of others who do not know God, or if we do not practice doing this, we are missing a huge part of what God has created us for.

When we worship, we are establishing God's throne. It is a differentiating factor of how we live compared to others who do not know God. I am not referring to a superficial "Praise the Lord" that comes not from the heart but has been learned through parroting. What I am speaking of is a sincere devotion in which worship flows from the heart.

God inhabits the praises of His people. God inhabits us through our vocalized worship. He inhabits us in such a way that the distinguishing mark in our lives becomes His presence. If we do not have this in our lives, we are falling far short of God's plan.

Jesus did nothing apart from the Father. Moses would not go into the Promised Land without God Himself going with him. David found his pleasures in the courts of God. This kind of intimate worship is necessary for us to live above superficiality, embracing a sincere heart of devotion to the Lord.

One time I had a dream, a throne room encounter, in which I saw the words of Revelation 4 in red as if soaked in blood. When I picked up one of my Bibles to read chapter 4, it was all red. Then I tried another Bible, and I saw the same thing! This was an eye-opening revelation that chapter 4 is about Jesus being the worthy one slain before the foundation of the world. It was also connected to how He is the only one worthy of our worship.

> After these things I looked, and behold, a door standing open in heaven. And the first voice which I heard was like a trumpet speaking with me, saying, "Come up here, and I will show you things which must take place after this."
>
> Revelation 4:1

At the beginning of Revelation 4, the "trumpet" said, "Come up here." John was caught up in the Spirit. When we find ourselves in a place of sensitivity to the Holy Spirit, we will experience more of the things of heaven, the activity around His throne. God's world is far different from the one we live in. For us to carry His life, we need an experience that comes from the realm of heaven. God desires to reveal Himself to us in ways that are far above this earthly plane.

God invites us to come and experience more of Him. All we have to do is simply respond to these invitations with a willing heart. The invitation is to whosoever will come, with no respecting of persons. To move into places of encounter, we do need an earnest desire with an authentic hunger for His presence. Spiritual hunger propels us into a place of encounter with the Lord. God is not boring; to the contrary, He is full of electricity, power and spiritual charge. Jesus calls us to be awake and ready that we may engage in the heart of what God is doing.

Oh, how we need the centrality of Jesus in our lives! When He is the central focus of our lives, everything flows in peaceful harmony. Regardless of what is going on around us, because we keep our eyes on Him, His peace rules over us. When Jesus is enthroned inside of us, He causes His peace to flow like a river through our lives. With God's peace within us, we have nothing to fear. When He is the center of our worship, tranquility rules, giving us overwhelming victory.

"The twenty-four elders fall down before Him who sits on the throne and worship Him who lives forever and ever, and cast their crowns before the throne" (Revelation 4:10). Here we see Jesus sitting on His throne, in a position of resting, because the work is finished. He is in the place of ultimate authority, ruling in righteousness—the King ruling over all creation. By His grace Jesus has given us priestly white robes of righteousness so that we are covered in His glory. The white garments represent being made clean and holy. His blood has washed us and covered us, and we are now worthy to stand in His presence because of His finished work on the cross. He has made us kings, giving us the privileged place to rule and reign with Him.

"Surely the Lord GOD does nothing, unless He reveals His secret to His servants the prophets" (Amos 3:7). Many have a lofty view of the role of prophet, but every true prophet begins as a person having intimacy with God. Even if someone has been called by God to be a prophet, if intimacy with God is never established, that person will only become a distorted image of what he or she was intended to walk in. A prophet is only as good as his (or her) time with God.

120

Manifest His Glory

"Arise, shine; for your light has come! And the glory of the LORD is risen upon you. . . . The LORD will arise over you, and His glory will be seen upon you" (Isaiah 60:1–2). While we are here on earth, we are called to establish God's throne where we are. Whenever we worship, pray, preach or engage in any activity of God's Kingdom, we do it so that God's authority and rule would be established in the hearts of people and in cities, regions and nations. Our role is to manifest His glory in such a way as to displace darkness with His light. God desires to use us so that heaven changes things on earth. When we walk in His presence, God's glory affects all that surrounds us.

An Excellent Spirit

"But My servant Caleb, because he has a different spirit in him and has followed Me fully, I will bring into the land where he went, and his descendants shall inherit it" (Numbers 14:24). Through our persistent faith, consistency in worship, intercession and acts of love, we expand the borders of the current realm of heaven on earth. We need to hold fast to God's call on our lives here rather than drifting aimlessly into things that are not fulfilling. Keeping focus gives us clarity of thought and accomplishment. Like Caleb, we need a "different spirit" that is exemplary in faith; for he who is born of God overcomes the world, possessing and inheriting the promises (see 1 John 5:4).

Our enemy, though, will not go quietly. "And he shall speak great words against the most High, and shall wear out the saints of the most High" (Daniel 7:25 KJV). Do not allow him to weary you, cause you to lose focus or bring you into an oppressive state of mind. Keep your eyes on God's perfect plan for being on the planet. Every day is an opportunity to affect the atmosphere where we are.

121

Jesus gave His life so that we would find freedom and then be able to be the conduits of His glory in the earth. He has given us His Holy Spirit to bear the fruit of righteousness in our lives. The Holy Spirit is the most powerful weapon that we have because He is the very person of God *inside* of us! It does not get any better than this! So live out your privilege of being a dwelling place for God. "For the kingdom of God is not eating and drinking, but righteousness and peace and joy in the Holy Spirit" (Romans 14:17).

There is an awakening in the Church in regard to life in the Holy Spirit, because we cannot overcome or glorify Jesus without Him. There is no way we can live without an intimate communion with the Spirit. When we learn the ways of God through the truth of His Word and dependence on His Spirit, His life and blessing will flow like a river.

Portals of Heaven

When I stumbled upon the phrase *portals of heaven*, I named one of my instrumental albums after it. The theme of the album was really referring to actual portals in the heavens. You can see them in the story of Jacob, when he saw the angels of God ascending and descending on the ladder to and from the heavens. "Then he dreamed, and behold, a ladder was set up on the earth, and its top reached to heaven; and there the angels of God were ascending and descending on it" (Genesis 28:12). The psalmist Asaph also talks about the supernatural activity that took place through "the doors of heaven" when God gave manna to His people. "Yet He had commanded the clouds above, and opened the doors of heaven, had rained down manna on them to eat, and given them of the bread of heaven" (Psalm 78:23–24).

God pours His blessings through open portals in the heavens. We ourselves are also doorways, gateways, portals of God's glory and substance. The tongue is the mode through which we release things in the spirit realm. You have experienced this; we all have, both the good and the bad. The words that we speak have substantial impact on people in both ways. What a responsibility we have to be releasers of the goodness of God into our respective atmospheres. How awesome a privilege! God has created us in such a way that we get to participate as a doorway for His goodness. His glory is revealed and made known through us.

"This beginning of signs Jesus did in Cana of Galilee, and manifested His glory; and His disciples believed in Him" (John 2:11). Jesus, during His earthly ministry, was the ultimate portal of heaven. As you read the gospels, you see heaven advancing into the earth through Him. His words were anointed of the Spirit, with miracles, deliverance and healing all being demonstrated in the earth. The Kingdom of God was coming on earth as it is in heaven, through Jesus. In the same way God fully intends to reveal Himself through us.

> Most assuredly, I say to you, he who believes in Me, the works that I do he will do also; and greater works than these he will do, because I go to My Father. And whatever you ask in My name, that I will do, that the Father may be glorified in the Son. If you ask anything in My name, I will do it.
>
> John 14:12–14

You are a doorway of heaven, just as Jesus is the Door. This is not something you become. This is who you are. It is not something that can be earned, but rather lived. Through your communion with God you are a vessel of God's presence and power to others. Jesus was the Son of God, yet He still had to spend time in the presence of the Father. Not only that, but He lived in constant communion with the Father. Should we pay any less a price? This life of devotion was essential in the life of Jesus. How much more does this apply to our lives? God has made you a portal that is specifically designed to manifest His glory. When we spend our devotion on Him, all that is left to do is "open the door" as portals of heaven to others.

Finding consistency in this is an important factor to keep us in a place of effectiveness for His glory. Our lives cannot be like teeter-totters that shift one way and then drift the other way. Divine focus, setting our eyes on the heart and will of God, is an essential element that steers us like the rudder does a ship into the place of consistent living before His presence. Imagine a ship that is constantly going off course. It may get back on course over and over again, but much time is wasted. That is why Paul tells us to run the race to win: "Do you not know that those who run in a race all run, but one receives the prize? Run in such a way that you may obtain it" (1 Corinthians 9:24). There is a way to run that brings us victory. It is not enough to be on the course; we must be on course the entire way. To the level that we maintain our focus, we will also maintain consistency in establishing the throne of God in the earth.

In the next chapter we will look more closely at what it means to live close to the heart of God.

Life Application

- **WHAT** atmospheres can you affect? Think of some of the common places that you go every day. What lives can be touched there?
- **THINK** about God on His throne. Take in the wonder of who He is and what He has done for you. Enter into a time of worship, exalting Him in the beauty of holiness.
- **PRAY** for the spirit of wisdom and revelation. God wants to open your eyes to see what He sees. When we get His perspective on things, it changes how we view things.
- **KNOW** that God wants you in on His plans. God searches the earth for those who are faithful to Him.

8

Prophets of Intimacy

But Samuel ministered before the Lord, even as a child, wearing a linen ephod.

1 Samuel 2:18

Samuel had an unusual devotional life with God. He continually experienced God's presence from a very early age. In the time he lived, the Bible says, the "word of the Lord was rare," and there was no "widespread revelation" (1 Samuel 3:1). What an interesting description. Apparently the nation as a whole had grown dull to the voice of God. The issue was not that God was not speaking but that people were not hearing. Even so, the Lord found a spirit of true worship being cultivated in Samuel's heart. He found someone who would spend time before His throne in worship. Because of Samuel's devotion, he developed an ear that could hear the voice of the Lord.

God had also found someone He could trust. Is it not as basic as that? Just as we develop trust in people we spend time with, learning their ways and character, so God looks for those He can trust because they value Him enough to spend time with

Him. That is the truest essence of a prophet. As we read on in 1 Samuel, we see that God entrusted Samuel with great authority to release the word of the Lord to the people, to correct Saul and to establish David as king of Israel.

Early on in my walk with God, my perception of a "prophet" of God reached somewhat lofty heights. The picture in my mind was quite extravagant. I tend to think that this is a common view for most. Generally speaking, either people do not believe prophets exist anymore or, if they do believe in modern-day prophets, they do not have a clear understanding of what that looks like. Then you have those who believe they are prophets but in most cases are not. At times titles are adopted by identity-starved people looking for something to make them feel valuable. But God knows who His prophets are.

In my walk with God, I have learned that some people are born with unusual supernatural gifting to see in the spirit realm or into the future, even though they may not follow God. Without a doubt those gifts can only be used for God's glory when a life has been given in devotion to Him. No matter if someone has a prophetic gift or is a prophet, outside of a true, intimate relationship with God, that person's life and works will count for nothing. Whether someone is born with a peculiar prophetic gift or learns to hear and see through faithfulness and intimacy with God—it makes no difference. Just as Samuel grew in God's presence, we also grow as we are faithful to spend our time with Him, learning to hear His voice and follow.

What Is a Prophet?

A prophet is someone who lives so close to God as to hear and feel the heart of God. As we become more intimate with God, He begins to show us what He is doing and saying. When we look at the prophetic life in these terms, we see that everyone is invited into this life: "Then Moses said to him, ' . . . Oh, that all the LORD's people were prophets and that the LORD would put His Spirit upon them!'" (Numbers 11:29). All of us are called to hear the voice of God, to know His heart concerning our lives and the world around us. In any relationship, how well we know a person is proportional to the time we spend with him or her. It is the same with God.

David was a king, psalmist, warrior and prophet. He is the picture of a man who had titles but never claimed any. He was not so presumptuous as to try to wrest the kingdom from Saul. Even when he had the chance to kill Saul and, in man's eyes, would have been justified in doing so, he would not. David took responsibility for his actions. Even when he was in the wrong—such as when he was confronted with his secret sin by the prophet Nathan—he was wise enough not to take things into his own hands. He did not retaliate (see 2 Samuel 12:1–23). Because David knew God in private, not only in public, he had the substance required to be a man after God's own heart. David valued God's presence more than anything; he knew how to get in God's presence, even though in at least one season he decided to leave. He still knew the way back. Since he had been a boy, he knew the way of worship. A heart of worship is not something that can be formulized; it is a way of life.

Spending Time with God

Spending time with God is the foundation for growing in the prophetic. You can spend time with someone in many different ways. All have value, and we cannot neglect quality time with one another if we are to know each other and have healthy relationships. Below I give you three pictures of how we spend time with God. When we are learning how to use our spiritual ears, hearing His voice and living as prophetic people, it helps to see the differences in the ways we can interact with God.

Recreation Time

Different ways that we spend time with our loved ones serve different purposes. When we spend recreation time with someone, we are doing nothing more than getting out and having a good time. There is no big agenda, just the enjoyment of the company—going to the park, playing a game, simply taking pleasure in valuable, fun interaction with one another. Believe it or not, God likes to have fun with us, for it is natural for a father to enjoy spending time with his family. The dysfunction in families these days means that many are deprived of this view of God. If you never had a father who had fun with you, you will most likely see a gap between your life experience and the quality recreation time that God would gladly engage in. This is why our perception of God is critically important. If we can learn to see Him as He really is, we will have many more joys we can enter into. "Then I will go to the altar of God, to God my exceeding joy" (Psalm 43:4).

Recreation means to "re-create." God is into renovations, renewals and re-creating our lives to be full of His life and Spirit. Do not ever sell yourself short of knowing God as a Father. Jesus Himself referred to God as His Father. The religious leaders could not understand this because they only knew the rituals of religion. Fun is part of relationships. If you do not have fun in your close relationships, they cannot grow. They may not even last. It pays to learn how to have fun, laugh a little and find that God really is good!

Heart Time

Heart time in a relationship is when both people slow down enough to really listen to one another at a deeper level. There is less to distract us from our conversation. Here we get to know each other better in a more intimate time together.

"Create in me a clean heart, O God, and renew a steadfast spirit within me. Do not cast me away from Your presence, and do not take Your Holy Spirit from me" (Psalm 51:10–11). In our heart times with God, we learn about Him—what He likes, what He wants and the things on His heart that are specific to our lives. God wants His people to spend time with Him so He can reveal His secrets to them. This requires heart-to-heart time. This is where we get quiet in His presence and commune with His Holy Spirit. It is a time when we rest in Him. We lay down our thoughts and ask Him what He would like to say to us. It is not the time for petitions or asking for what we want. Rather we lay all of our questions down for the one thing He would like to say. It may be His voice telling you of His love for you. Sometimes it is that simple. Sometimes He will point out things needing correction in our hearts to bring cleansing and forgiveness. Without this time we can grow very superficial in our lives, losing true substance in our relationship with Him.

Work Time

Work time is when people do things together, working together for a specific goal that needs to be accomplished and seeing it happen together. Most people are well acquainted with this type of relationship; yet recreation time and heart time are what make your work time fruitful. We can avoid lots of frustration by simply prioritizing our fun and heart time before the work time. Our work is only as productive as the time we spend with Him. By engaging in the other forms of quality time, we will not leave Him behind. He will be with us in our work with blessing and increase, bringing an overflow.

"And [Jesus] said to them, 'Why did you seek Me? Did you not know that I must be about My Father's business?'" (Luke 2:49). When you read this verse in the biblical Greek, the word *business* is not there. The verse really reads, "I must be about my Father." The New King James Version and other translations add the word *business*, *house* or something else. The meaning of this is beautiful; it paints intimacy with God as the core substance that made the work of Jesus full of the Father's purpose.

131

We interact with God in all of these ways. They are not religious formulas but rather relational approaches, no different from the way we approach our other relationships. Knowing that God desires a relationship with us in all three spheres—recreation, heart and work—will help us engage with Him in every aspect of our lives and grow our ability to hear Him as a prophetic people.

Against the Grain

Prophets are trumpets of the voice of God. They are to declare clearly God's heart concerning things. Trumpets have a distinct and clear sound and were used to call armies together, awakening the people to a purpose. The Lord needs those who have a pure-hearted relationship with Him, without ulterior motives, so that when they blow the trumpet, what emerges is a clear sound. When motives are mixed, it muddies the sound so that it is not clearly distinguishable.

The prophet Samuel had a clear voice. None of his words fell to the ground (see 1 Samuel 3:19). There was no compromise in his heart. He lived in an intimate communion with God that kept his heart pure. God is looking for more people to embrace such a life of intimacy that when He speaks, it is not filtered through opinion, preference and performance.

One of the notable characteristics of people without compromise is that they tend to go against the grain of what is commonly accepted as the norm. People pleasing is not an option for them. The life of Jesus shows the same thing; the things He did and said came as an offense to the religious crowd.

When you go against the grain on a piece of wood, it is much harder to do. When you swim against the current of a river, it takes all your strength to cross to the other side. It is always easy to take the path of least resistance—the popular path. Against the grain is a *cross*current. God calls us to embrace the cross. This is the painful and difficult path, not the primrose path. Yet this was the life that Jesus lived. He did not promote "country club" Christianity. On the contrary, such people were the kind of people that He offended.

For us to overflow with His presence, we will encounter crossroads of decision. These decision points will determine whether we will take the easy road to please man or the harder road that pleases God. We do not need to go out of our way to find these opportunities, so we need not make them happen on our own. But as we follow the Lord, it is inevitable that we will encounter choices that will offend even those closest to us. God will make sure of it. Why? He knows that if we are not able to handle the smallest bit of pain from how others perceive us, then He will not be able to trust us with what He considers a greater call for our lives.

He who is faithful with little will be entrusted with much. If we cannot be faithful with the small decisions, He will not promote us to bigger tasks. God does want to promote us. But not without a price. God looks for faithfulness and rewards it. Sometimes people get prematurely promoted in the natural, and God allows it but does not endorse it; then they fall on their faces because their roots were too shallow.

God likes to build some grit in our lives that does not mind the opinions of man. Our hearts need a steadfast focus on His thoughts, valuing them more than anything else in this world. When we have this kind of heart, we will not mind going against the grain of what is accepted by the majority.

The Many Faces of God's Word

Scripture describes two fundamental ways that God's Word comes to us: the *logos* Word and the *rhema* word. *Logos* refers

133

to the revealed thoughts and will of God as recorded in Scripture; it is also a title for Jesus Himself in John 1. *Rhema* is a spoken word from God that comes to us in a particular time for a particular reason. God uses both of these to speak to us, and they both manifest in various forms. As a prophetic people, we want to learn to hear God's voice in any way it might appear. All the faces of God's Word that I describe below apply to the written Word as well as to the *rhema* word of God.

God's Word Is Light

"Your word is a lamp to my feet and a light to my path" (Psalm 119:105). God's Word is light to us, opening up our eyes to see the truth and guiding us along the path of righteousness and life. Without the Word of God we are left in the darkness of deception. Jesus warned in John 3:19 that the reason people fail to come to Him is because they love darkness more than the light. As believers we run to the light of God's Word and truth, that we may grow into Him as true disciples.

God's Word Is the Rock

"Therefore whoever hears these sayings of Mine, and does them, I will liken him to a wise man who built his house on the rock" (Matthew 7:24). The Word is stability to our lives. Without it we will be blown back and forth by the winds of teaching. God's Word gives us solid ground to build our lives upon. I can remember a time when I was young and I went out on a boat with a group of people. When they decided to move to another part of the boat, it became unstable and flipped over. The result was that everyone got wet! Thankfully the Word of God is stable. No matter what anyone else does, it does not change, so it gives us solid footing, a sure and safe place to stand.

God's Word Is the Sword of the Spirit

"And take the helmet of salvation, and the sword of the Spirit, which is the word of God" (Ephesians 6:17). The Word is one of the spiritual weapons we have been given to fight the enemy of our souls. Some of its power lies in the fact that it can keep us in the will of God. Just as Jesus quoted the Word during His temptation in the wilderness, so we should store His Word in our hearts, so that when we are tempted, God's Word is within us to give us victory. "Your word I have hidden in my heart, that I might not sin against You" (Psalm 119:11).

God's Word Is a Fire and Hammer

"'Is not My word like a fire?' says the LORD, 'and like a hammer that breaks the rock in pieces?'" (Jeremiah 23:29). When God's words are like a fire in our hearts, we burn with passion to do the will of God. It holds the power of breakthrough for our lives. Whatever resistance there may be within us, God's Word is more powerful, taking out every hindrance to His desires. His Word breaks down the things in our hearts that are contrary to the Spirit, exposing and purifying us for His purposes.

God's Word Separates Soul and Spirit

"For the word of God is living and powerful, and sharper than any two-edged sword, piercing even to the division of soul and spirit, and of joints and marrow, and is a discerner of the thoughts and intents of the heart" (Hebrews 4:12). Our hearts are penetrated by God's words, allowing us to discern that which originates from our own flesh and self from that which is of His Spirit. The spirit man is fed by God's words that awaken our lives to His presence. Through it we see clearly our own motives for the things that we do, whether good or bad.

God's Word Is God Inspired

All Scripture is given by inspiration of God, and is profitable for doctrine, for reproof, for correction, for instruction in righteousness, that the man of God may be complete, thoroughly equipped for every good work.

2 Timothy 3:16–17

The Holy Spirit breathed upon men of God to write the Scriptures. The Word of God is holy and useful for making us effective in our walks with God. I can remember many times, when I first came to Jesus, that the Holy Spirit spoke verses to me before I had even read them or knew them. The Holy Spirit makes God's Word alive in our hearts. He will come to open the eyes of our understanding to see His truth clearly.

God's Word Is Healing

"He sent His word and healed them, and delivered them from their destructions" (Psalm 107:20). Healing power is also in the Word. In His earthly ministry, all Jesus did, it seems, was heal, deliver and work miracles. He told His disciples that when they saw Him, they had seen the Father. It was God's will to heal then, and it is still His will to heal today, for Jesus Christ is the same yesterday, today and forever (see Hebrews 13:8). His Word is truth, so we can stand on His promise that the works Jesus did, we have the ability by His Spirit to do as well.

God's Word Upholds All Things

Who being the brightness of His glory and the express image of His person, and upholding all things by the word of His power, when He had by Himself purged our sins, sat down at the right hand of the Majesty on high.

Hebrews 1:3

Amazingly, the Word of God holds all things together. When God spoke, "Let there be light" (Genesis 1:3), light was created, and it still remains. When we allow God to speak into our lives personally, His words hold us together, giving us a peace and stability for our lives. Instead of us being scattered, He makes us whole and complete, strong and sure—giving us hope as an anchor for our souls (see Hebrews 6:19).

Jesus Is the Word of God

"And the Word became flesh and dwelt among us, and we beheld His glory, the glory as of the only begotten of the Father, full of grace and truth" (John 1:14). God's Word has such importance that Jesus Himself is called "the Word of God," the Word made flesh. Knowing that Jesus is synonymous with the Word should give us a great respect, priority and holy awe for it. In the psalms it states that God has exalted His Word above His own name (see Psalm 138:2). This is a huge statement. Jesus also told us that though heaven and earth will pass away, His words will remain.

God's Word Is the Final Authority

God's Word is the final authority for our lives. Take some time to really stop and see what the Lord thinks about your life—not what everybody else thinks, but the Lord. Forget all the false weights and measures of man's opinions of you. For many people the question is whether or not they can distinguish between the opinions of man and the Lord's thoughts. This is why it is so important for us to know what God's Word says about us. His Word is the standard.

Once you are saved, does the Lord view you as a sinner or a saint? Many have not crossed over into the simple truth that they are saints. Paul never addressed the "sinners" in Colossae or Philippi, only the saints. This is what the Word of God says about us.

How real is His righteousness, the righteousness of God, in your life? Only false humility exalts one's own failings. We should be giving credit to God for His overwhelming grace that makes us overcome.

Mindsets rooted in the sin nature show us how much we need to know what God thinks about us. His Word reveals this: He sees us as sons and daughters, not slaves. We have been adopted, not rejected. Only God, not the world, judges us. All of these little things make a difference in our thinking as believers. Are we believers or doubters? God calls us believers.

What does your family tree say about you? You have been grafted into a new family. What does God's lineage say about you? Whatever other people say about you, God says better things.

Whom do you want to identify with? What is your identity based on? Many people find their identity in what they do, instead of who they are in Christ. We need to be rooted and grounded in His thoughts about us. Make a fresh commitment to His Word in your life today.

The Word of God is our solid foundation to build upon as we venture into a prophetic life. To be a prophetic person is not to be strange, without the substance of God's Word. Rather, we are to be a people of encounters with God who have strong roots of understanding His truth as revealed in His Word. By marrying intimate experiences with God with the living Word, we grow healthy with His life and presence.

God is looking for prophets. He is looking for those who want to be like His Son, the Prophet of prophets. The prophetic life is not something to run from but to run to. As we learn to dwell in God's presence, developing a hearing ear, we are also carriers of His glory, with the ability to transform atmospheres and spiritual climates.

Life Application

- **WHY** does God value and associate Himself with prophets? Empty your mind of all of your experiences with the "prophetic" and do a word study on *prophetic* and *prophets* in the Bible to discover why God values His people embracing a prophetic life.

- **SPEND** alone time with God. See if you notice a difference in your relationship with Him and how much more clearly you hear His voice.

- **FIND** grace to be willing to go against the grain. God values those who are not "common" vessels but are willing to follow His direction regardless of the thoughts of others.

- **ALLOW** the Word of God to be your standard. Do not pick and choose verses that you favor, but ask God to open your heart to the fullness of His Word in truth.

9

The Gravity of His Glory

> And it came to pass, when the priests came out of
> the holy place, that the cloud filled the house of
> the LORD, so that the priests could not continue
> ministering because of the cloud; for the glory of
> the LORD filled the house of the LORD.
>
> 1 Kings 8:10–11

Some years ago I had a dream in which the Holy Spirit spoke to me in a worship meeting about the glory of His presence being like "gravity"—the gravity of God, pulling all things to Him. In this encounter everyone in the place was experiencing the weight of His presence. People were drawn into this realm of heaven, the weighty presence of God. God's gravity keeps us where we need to be, just as the sun holds the planets in their proper orbits. His glory is His realm of life released in our midst. I had never heard His glory described in this way, and it amazed me.

Maybe you have experienced this. God's glory is so real that it has an impact on our physical bodies; we can actually feel His glory in such a way that we want to rest or lie down because of the heaviness. A couple came to an event where the glory of God's presence was very thick and heavy. This was the first time they had experienced an event like this. When they went home afterward, they slept for three hours. They kept going back to more services, and after each one they did the same thing, sleeping for long periods. This had never happened to them before. The atmosphere of His glory brings such amazing peace, rest and refreshing that it manifests in our physical bodies.

Atmospheric Transformation

When Jesus told His disciples to pray for God's Kingdom to come on earth as it is in heaven, He was speaking of the very *atmosphere* of heaven being manifested in the earth. As believers we have the power to shift spiritual atmospheres. The Lord said to my wife in a dream once, "How does it feel to be responsible for the atmosphere of a city?" All over the earth are spiritual climates in drought for the presence of God. He is looking for people who understand His heart to cover His earth with the glory of His presence. "For the earth will be filled with the knowledge of the glory of the LORD, as the waters cover the sea" (Habakkuk 2:14). Through the Holy Spirit we have the ability to change spiritual climates, flooding the earth with His glory. We need to know the part we play in affecting the earth with His glory, because He will not be doing it without us.

Did you know that you yourself carry a spiritual climate? God's plan is to fill you with heaven's glory, His atmosphere. Everyone experiences various spiritual climates from being around people each day. The glory of God's presence is greater than any other climate you come in contact with. In our worship and devotion we have the opportunity to overflow, with the love and presence of His Spirit affecting those around us.

We have much more authority than we realize. God has given us different kinds of weapons to change spiritual climates. Wherever darkness is, we carry the light of God to expose it, displace it and cast it out. We need to be committed to carrying His light as dwelling places of God. His glory and presence dwelling in our lives displace darkness. As carriers of His glory we can walk into places and change the atmosphere. Oppression cannot dwell where His glory invades, for it is the substance of heaven, the weight of heaven's realm that pushes oppressive darkness out of the way.

The glory is God Himself. The Holy Spirit is the Person of the Godhead who is most representative of God's presence and glory. He is called "the Spirit of glory": "If you are reproached for the name of Christ, blessed are you, for *the Spirit of glory* and of God rests upon you" (1 Peter 4:14, emphasis added).

God's glory is the weight and realm of heaven manifested by the Holy Spirit. It is something that we actually feel on our bodies. It is experiential. When Jesus was on the Mount of Transfiguration, the glory of God descended upon the mountain at its highest level. This must have been the pinnacle of intense glory on earth. Peter, James and John were amazed and awestruck by the glory of God that manifested. They literally did not know what to do with it, though Peter came up with some ideas. He was ready to plant a church on the mountain. But God was not about to let him confine His glory in boxed-in thinking. The Father corrected Peter, saying, "Listen to My Son!" The glory of God is that tangible, that awesome and amazing. Peter just did not know what to do with it.

The glory of the Lord will cover the earth as the waters cover the sea. God has destined us to be the carriers of His most excellent glory throughout the earth. He is going to fill this earth with His glory through the Church of His presence. It is His glory that changes atmospheres, ushering in the realm of heaven.

At a conference some years ago, there was a very powerful atmosphere of God's glory in the meeting. The person ministering came up to me with oil in his hands that had the fragrance of roses. The oil was not something he had poured into his hands; rather it came out of his hands from being in God's glory. It was an awesome, heavenly fragrance. Another time I was in the basement of a church where God's presence was very strong after a meeting. Before we knew what was happening, golden glitter covered the tops of the tables where we were eating lunch. These are just some of the things that happen when His glory and presence are strong. Sometimes miracles and healings are manifestations of the glory of His presence, and all these things can happen at the same time.

The reason we are on the planet is to be ushers of His glory in the earth, fulfilling the prayer of Jesus that His Kingdom would come on earth. People will experience God through us. It is good to invite people to church, but at some point we also have to realize that we are carriers of His glory, holding the power to transform lives right where we are.

The Weighty *Kabod*

In the Bible we see that God's glory was manifested in such a way that the priests were not able to minister any longer. The weight of glory in God's presence became too strong for them to stand.

> Indeed it came to pass, when the trumpeters and singers were as one, to make one sound to be heard in praising and thanking the LORD, and when they lifted up their voice with the trumpets and cymbals and instruments of music, and praised the LORD,

saying: "For He is good, for His mercy endures forever," that the house, the house of the LORD, was filled with a cloud, so that the priests could not continue ministering because of the cloud; for the glory of the LORD filled the house of God.

2 Chronicles 5:13–14

In the Hebrew, the word for glory is *kabod*, and its definition is the "weighty" presence of the Lord. Have you ever experienced the weight of His glory in worship? If you have, you know that this is the way to live. Anything less than this comes up short. Receiving a heart of worship, we can enter into greater realms of His glory. We can experience more of His weighty presence through worship.

It is the will of God for us to experience His glory every day. This is not something high and lofty or out of reach, but rather is included in the blessing package of God's overflowing love. His glory is accessible to us as inheritors of God's blessings and benefits. "Let the saints be joyful in glory [*kabod*]: let them sing aloud on their beds" (Psalm 149:5). When we begin to live in the place of His weighty glory, we then experience more of His life and desires. His glory is the place we tangibly connect with Him. There really is no formula to it. When our hearts are hungry for God, it does not take much to get us in the place of experiencing His presence. Jesus told us that if we hunger and thirst for righteousness, we shall be filled. With our hunger in place, here are a few things that can translate that hunger into a living experience with God.

Strongly Vocalize Your Worship

"Blessed are the people who know the joyful sound! They walk, O LORD, in the light of Your countenance" (Psalm 89:15). You want to sense the river of life flowing out in your worship. You want to release the sound. This does not mean you have to shout, although that is permissible, but volume makes a difference. You have heard it said, "Turn up the volume!" At times we just need to turn up the volume of our worship to God. Understand that the devil does not like your voice when it is consecrated to God. He does not want to hear you. He also does not want you to fill the atmosphere of the earth with praise to God.

"But thou art holy, O thou that inhabitest the praises of Israel" (Psalm 22:3 KJV). When we praise, God inhabits that praise. In turn, He inhabits us. When we turn up the volume of our worship, we are also releasing boldness inside of us. It is a good thing when we do not care what other people think. We need to honor the Lord before men. God is first; when we put Him first in all things, He cannot help but bless us.

It is not always about the words but rather directing your sound to God. You do not need words to worship. You can make a joyful sound instead: "Make a joyful shout to God, all the earth!" (Psalm 66:1). The more you can get the sound from within your spirit, the better. Obviously you *can* use words. I love to use the name of Jesus and any other words that come in the flow of heart worship. It is also good to sing in the Spirit, pray in tongues, sing in tongues and even groan in the Spirit at times. You want to feel the spirit of worship flowing toward God from within yourself. In worship is the weight of His glory.

Worship until You Sense a Saturation

Worship for some time before the Lord. Realize that worship is all about the Lord, but in the process you benefit. In our worship we should sense the blessing of God coming upon us. This is the point when He begins to pour out His weighty presence upon us. Welcome Him to come in this way. Also realize that it is the Holy Spirit filling you in your worship. Ask the Holy Spirit to fill you more.

What does it mean to be saturated? Think of food that is marinated over time. In our family kitchen, we sometimes prepare meat this way for a stir-fry. When we marinate the beef in teriyaki sauce, the garlic and spices saturate with the oil to tenderize and flavor the meat. When we spend time getting saturated in the Holy Spirit, we are allowing Him to tenderize us so that we will taste good (spiritually) to others. Just as Scripture tells us to taste and see the Lord is good, we should have a flavor in our lives that draws people to God as well. The element of time makes all the difference. All that beef does in that time is sit in the saturation until it takes on the flavor of the ingredients. Time in God's presence makes a huge difference in how we look, feel and taste spiritually. Many times people want results without taking the time to see those results. We cannot expect something for nothing. The saying is true: You get what you pay for. Take time to saturate yourself in the Holy Spirit. Our salvation is free, but we are rewarded for daily sacrifice motivated by the pure desire of knowing and obeying Him.

Prepare to Receive in the Place of Saturation

In a place of sensing the saturation of the Spirit, do not rush to the next thing. Move in and out of worship to God; give and receive. The Lord will begin to speak to you things that you need to hear. This is the Holy Spirit coming in wisdom and revelation. "However, when He, the Spirit of truth, has come, He will guide you into all truth; for He will not speak on His own authority, but whatever He hears He will speak; and He will tell you things to come" (John 16:13).

Stay in a place of sensitivity, allowing Him to speak. Then write down what you are hearing. Stop and worship a little more, then hear more, worship a little more, then hear more, write more, etc. We live in a day when most people like to speak but are not all that good at listening. Learn to slow down to hear the voice of God. What impressions are you getting as you sense His presence upon you? Is there a song in your heart, a melody or something coming to mind in the form of an idea? Do not be too quick to discard what may not seem "spiritual"; many times God gives us ideas, wisdom and songs to help us in our lives in practical ways.

Carry God's Presence

You can continue in this throughout the day by maintaining a heart of worship and sensitivity to the Holy Spirit. He will show you things to record and things to do to bless others. It is a very powerful thing to be connected to the Holy Spirit in such an intimate way. This is how we experience being the most highly blessed people, by having this awesome communication with God. Because we are blessed in this way, we are then able to be a blessing to other people. As we go out, we can pour out on others.

At one point in my life, I would walk around with a small tape recorder to make sure that I was catching what He was speaking to me, either in words or songs. This helped me stay close in His presence as I went through the day. Even to this day I use the recorder on my mobile phone to capture things God gives to me. It is a great tool for keeping engaged in His presence. God has lots of good things to share with us to help us know Him better; we can even share those experiences with others. God wants us to overflow with the goodness of His presence wherever we go.

Practice Intercessory Worship

There is a place in worship where we are carrying a heart of intercession along with lifting up the Lord. Romans speaks of intercessory groanings that are too intense for words (see Romans 8:26). When we have the weight of intercession behind what we are singing, it becomes more than a song. The power of the Spirit is released into the atmosphere to bring about a change, a shift in the atmosphere.

"And I will pour on the house of David and on the inhabitants of Jerusalem the Spirit of grace and supplication" (Zechariah 12:10). When a life of worship becomes endowed with a spirit of prayer, the weight of worship becomes much more powerful in effect. It is one thing to worship with words, but when a spirit of prayer is part of the foundation of the worship, a greater weight comes upon the worship. A life of intercession creates a force in our worship that transcends the singing of a song. Within the sound is embedded a power of God that is released to break through demonic atmospheres.

As people of prayer, interceding before the Lord, God puts His weight behind our words because we are not operating out of the natural mind but by the intercession of the Spirit within us. Intercessory worship breaks open the way for God's manifested presence to come in powerfully.

This is a merging of two powerful weapons of the Spirit into one. Worship takes us higher; intercession with prophetic decree breaks open the atmosphere for God's glory. Understanding that Jesus lives forever to make intercession for the saints, we should desire to embrace an intercessory heart.

How do we obtain this kind of heart? We simply need to ask the Lord to fill us with this grace for intercession and worship. Everything that we receive is a gift from God. Through faithfulness we grow in what God has given us, but all is freely given. By use we learn to walk in what He has entrusted to us: "But solid food belongs to those who are of full age, that is, those who *by reason of use* have their senses exercised to discern both good and evil" (Hebrews 5:14, emphasis added).

Release the Power of Sound

We are flooded with sound from every direction, and it is a powerful force. The world is drawn to the sound of seduction, which is only a counterfeit of the sound of the voice of God. His voice has much more power, but that power can only be realized through a people of pure devotion, prayer and worship.

"His feet were like fine brass, as if refined in a furnace, and His voice as the sound of many waters" (Revelation 1:15). The Lord comes in the sound of many waters that goes throughout the earth. In the beginning God created through the sound of His voice. Heaven and hell both have sounds of their own; God wants to use the sound of His realm to change things on the earth. We are taught in Proverbs 18:21 that our words have the power of life and death. The sound we are releasing is extremely important to God. As we are filled with the sound of life, we impart life to those hearing, and the anointed sound that is released changes atmospheres. This is how the Holy Spirit overflows in our lives, affecting people and atmospheres.

It really does not take as much as we might think. When we look at the size and enormity of the world, it can be a little much to believe that we can have such a powerful effect. But in the life of Jesus, we see the impact one person can have, shifting the history of the world. By His Spirit we can have an impact when we vocalize the heart and sound of heaven.

Jesus had an impact not only because of His vocalization of the Father's heart but because the actions that accompanied it sealed everything He said forever. His actions made His words go further. It is one thing to say something; it is another to do it. He was God in the flesh, emptied of His divine powers. He was empowered as a man with the Holy Spirit. He set the example for us, showing us what a lasting effect we can have through the power of His Spirit within us.

Jesus said the words that He spoke were life (see John 6:63). With words filled with His life, we can also release a sound that carries the weight of heaven behind it, transforming atmospheres.

Biblical Examples of God's Glory

In the Garden of Eden, Adam and Eve were clothed in the glory of God, heaven on earth until the fall of man. Supernatural events such as the visitations that Abraham had were God's glory revealed. Where Jacob saw angels ascending and descending the ladder to heaven was a place where God's glory was being manifested on earth.

The wonders performed in Egypt that delivered the children of Israel, the parting of the Red Sea, the burning bush before which Moses took off his sandals and many more miraculous events throughout the Bible were tokens of God's glory demonstrated in the earth. Every wonder, miracle, healing and deliverance that Jesus performed was a demonstration of God's glory. Peter described the glory of God manifested at the Transfiguration as the "Excellent Glory" (2 Peter 1:17). He witnessed Moses, Elijah and Jesus together with the glory of heaven surrounding them, a moment not to be missed. This was the highest level of glory that Peter had seen, experienced or felt—yet Peter had also seen all the works that Jesus had done. This puts things in perspective!

Various Manifestations of His Glory

The glory of God manifests in a multitude of ways, but in most every case that I have experienced, a weight of His presence comes with His glory. Once I had a dream in which the manifested glory of His presence came into a prayer room. Suddenly there were manifestations of heaven on my bed that were indescribable. I turned to see angel feathers all over the walls, and floating in the air was an orb of God's glory. I was amazed, for I could see universes inside of it. The encounter was so powerful that in the dream I wanted to capture it on my iPhone. As I attempted to take the picture, my phone began to melt because the glory was so strong! The point of this dream was to show me that the kind of glory God is going to pour out cannot be captured and promoted by man, because it will be His work, and He will take care of letting others know.

In another encounter I was standing in a church service, and golden glory like rain was falling down. Then a purple glory cloud entered the room, as well as an angel who was bringing supernatural multiplication of finances. Before this encounter, our family was in a transition and had need of finances. The Lord had shown us where we were to move, but we did not have the money to get there. We trusted that the Lord would make the way. One day after my encounter in church, my wife came to me with a puzzled look on her face. She found in our bank account $10,000 more than what should have been there. We checked into it to make sure we had not missed a payment or that there was some type of error. But no—amazingly, God had put this money in our account. We do not know how or where it came from. He is Jehovah-Jireh! He really can make a way when there is no way.

I have been in many meetings when the weighty glory of His presence came and people experienced the fire of God upon their bodies, being healed of health issues. With the glory comes the reality of "as it is in heaven." Since there is no sickness in heaven, people will be healed. In most every case, worship opens the way for the glory; then heaven begins to manifest.

One time in a dream I experienced God's glory in the form of electricity in heaven. I was lying on a cloud, simultaneously in two places on the extreme ends of this cloud. The light of

God's glory came flowing from my left hand and arched in rainbow form to my right hand, where I lay on the opposite side of the cloud. God's glory was a brilliant white light in this rainbow arch. It was like being caught up in an electric field, where the charge of God's presence was the most powerful thing imaginable. His glory is power that causes miraculous events to take place. Over and over Scripture talks of how God has displayed His glory through His wonders and miracles. This is to be normal life for the believer.

In worship meetings where God has manifested His glory, people just like to stay and hang out, because there is nothing more satisfying to the soul than being in the presence of God's glory. The glory of God has manifested in the form of golden oil, rain, a cloud and many other ways. What we need to understand is that, though God is not limited in how He can manifest His glory, it will always have the fingerprint of heaven on it; it will not defy His nature as revealed biblically.

Beginning to walk in God's glory can be such an experience that some may neglect maintenance of good biblical foundations. In the next chapter we will shore up some fundamentals that keep us rooted in God's wisdom.

Life Application

- **BE** an atmosphere changer! Learn to be conscious of God's presence, knowing that His glory can change any atmosphere to conform to His heavenly standard.

- **PRACTICE** entering into God's presence through worship. God inhabits the praise of His people. Jesus paid the highest price for you to experience Him, not just know Him intellectually.

- **MAKE** a joyful sound! Turn up the volume in your worship. You will find it a place of personal breakthrough for your life and the lives of others. When we do this, we are changing the atmosphere to be "as it is in heaven."

10

Foundational Thinking

> If the foundations are destroyed, what can the righteous do?
>
> Psalm 11:3

Without a good foundation, we cannot build anything that will last. In our pursuit of God's presence we have to lay spiritual foundations that will form our lives at the ground level. Whether we are building our lives to give God glory or influencing the world in practical ways on behalf of the Kingdom of God, we need a solid foundation that is laid with His truth.

God is the one who designs the blueprints from which we build. We do not want to build on the wisdom of man but the wisdom that comes from God. This is why we need to abide in Him, seek to know His ways and pursue Him with a whole heart. We do not want to be shooting stars but people of light that shine for eternity: "But the path of the just is like the shining sun, that shines ever brighter unto the perfect day" (Proverbs 4:18).

God desires to bring us to a place where we find rest in Him, where all that we do flows from a life connected to His Spirit. When we learn to abide in Him, then the inspiration of the Holy Spirit is available to lead us and guide us into all truth. He gives us divine inspiration with right foundations of thinking on which to build.

We are all called to follow God and to lead others in our spheres of influence. Every day we have an opportunity to set the right example for someone and lead that person in the right direction. We lead according to the example given by those we respect. Our goal is to be numbered among the good leaders, not the bad, and good leaders have good foundations. As leaders, whether of multitudes or a few, we must have a foundation formed through faithfulness in time we spend with God.

If our foundation is not genuine but superficial and cheaply made, what we attempt to accomplish will eventually fall apart. The initial excitement might sustain us for a while, but the test is in the longevity of our work. Having a good foundation is a way of ensuring a good future. Here are some of the essential things we must have in place to form a good foundation.

Our Identity

Where we find our identity is paramount, no matter who we are—but even more so for leaders. If we find our identity in numbers of people, gifting, titles, accomplishments or anything other than a relationship with God, we are destined to make a mess of things. Our identity can only be found in Christ. We can do nothing to add to what He has done. Our absolute dependency on Him is a must if we are to have any longevity for the Kingdom of God.

Jesus made it clear that apart from the Father He could do nothing. Imagine that—God in the flesh Himself, confessing

His absolute dependency on His Father. How presumptuous some can be to think that they can make things work in their own strength, with their own programs, without having a heart that seeks the Lord! As I wrote in chapter 1, Moses had the wisdom to know better than to step out and do even what God had called him to do without having God's presence go with Him:

> "Now therefore, I pray, if I have found grace in Your sight, show me now Your way, that I may know You and that I may find grace in Your sight. And consider that this nation is Your people."
>
> And He said, "My Presence will go with you, and I will give you rest."
>
> Then he said to Him, "If Your Presence does not go with us, do not bring us up from here."
>
> Exodus 33:13–15

We need to make sure we have this kind of wisdom. It is Kingdom common sense to depend on the presence of God in order to succeed in what He has called us to.

Ancient Pillars

In a vision God showed me four ancient pillars: righteousness, grace, humility and wisdom. These pillars had the look of ancient trees, beautiful in glory and appearance. I could see what looked like a mist of glory covering them. It was very much like peering through something ancient, a glory covering of God's presence, and finding a treasure hidden inside. This is connected to our experiencing a continual flow of God's presence in our lives. Pillars are supports and must have great substance and strength. Because of this, the pillar is used to bring stability, help and strength. When these four pillars are in place, trust is established between you and God.

The Pillar of Righteousness

"Righteousness and justice are the foundation of Your throne; mercy and truth go before Your face" (Psalm 89:14). Righteousness was the first pillar that I saw. It means to walk in what is right, doing the right things. It is the very foundation of God's throne. This ancient pillar has nothing to do with our mere actions or self-righteousness; rather righteous actions flow out of our devotion to Him.

Doing what is right is not the same as doing what looks good. The Lord is looking for righteousness that is revealed inside out. Sometimes He will ask us to do things that do not look good from the spectator's standpoint. For instance, when Jesus healed on the Sabbath, He was purposely violating what was acceptable in the eyes of men in that day. Rebuking the religious leaders and calling them hypocrites did not make Him popular, either. People hold dear many sacred cows as "the way" things must be done. The good news is that God does not want us trapped in this box. He is about His business, not the business of what is religiously accepted.

Often God offends those who have a "small town" mindset because He sees the entire world. When you follow the Lord, people will be offended because of distorted expectations. The religious leaders in Jesus' day wanted a Messiah who would do what they wanted and expected. But the Lord has strong words for people pleasers: "Woe to you when all men speak well of you, for so did their fathers to the false prophets" (Luke 6:26). Here Jesus associates people pleasers with false prophets!

Envy was the reason the religious leaders crucified Jesus. He would not do things according to their expectations or yield to their presumption and control. He went against the grain of what they wanted and expected. Jesus told us that we have a cross to take up. A big part of this cross is being willing to follow God in such a way that some enemies turn up in the process.

The Pillar of Grace

"But by the grace of God I am what I am, and His grace toward me was not in vain; but I labored more abundantly than they all, yet not I, but the grace of God which was with me" (1 Corinthians 15:10). We see how important grace is as a foundation for our lives through the letters of Paul. Paul opens most every letter with "Grace and peace be to you from our Lord Jesus Christ." God's grace is extremely important for our lives if we are to grow up correctly into God's purposes. Not having grace as a foundation affects everything we do. Our view of God and of others is distorted without a proper understanding of grace.

"The grace of the Lord Jesus Christ, and the love of God, and the communion of the Holy Spirit be with you all. Amen" (2 Corinthians 13:14). The Greek word for grace in this verse, *charis*, means graciousness, in particular the divine influence upon the heart and its reflection in one's life in the form of gratitude. God's grace is the divine influence upon the heart. Most have heard about grace only by the definition "unmerited favor." It is by grace that we are saved through faith, the gift of God. But the grace of God also influences our hearts in such a way that His presence transforms us.

Jesus said that he who is forgiven much loves much. In other words, he who has experienced much grace shows much grace. When we experience God's love and forgiveness, we realize the depth to which we have been forgiven; in this we are able to have a greater grace in our hearts for others. When we experience God's grace, the "chip on the shoulder" is knocked off, for we realize that if not for God's grace we would be no better off than any other.

"For the law was given through Moses, but grace and truth came through Jesus Christ" (John 1:17). Jesus was full of grace and truth, not the law and a critical spirit. When people are

159

hard on others, it is a sign that they need more grace in their hearts, more divine influence, for man is selfish by nature. It is possible for someone to taste of God's love and grace and not give it away. But we want to enter into the fullness of His grace. We are called to be dispensers of the grace of God.

The longer I live the more aware I am that grace is what I need. We have to realize that if we are standing, it is only by the grace of God. The moment we think that we can do God's business apart from Him, working independently of Him, we will fall. It is His grace that works in us for His good pleasure.

It is always good to stir our minds to remember His grace. In this there is a safeguard for us: As long as we stay dependent on His grace, seeking His face, we are in a safe place.

The Pillar of Humility

An assault on humility has been unleashed in our day. Because of the dysfunction of the family unit, even among churchgoers, large portions of several generations have taken on a heart of rebellion. Understandably, many have fallen into this course of life because of a dire lack of godly examples for living. The unfulfilled need for true fathers has created a void in the lives of too many. With the degradation of values in numerous streams of Christianity, many have a view of the Church as a body of hypocrites whose lives do not express the truths they espouse. Many who claim to follow God live a humdrum life, with no heart desire for intimacy, substance or depth in relationship with Him. We must dedicate ourselves to recapturing the heart of humility, a dependency on His Spirit accompanied by transparency and honesty.

Humility is better walked out than talked about. "Now the man Moses was very humble, more than all men who were on the face of the earth" (Numbers 12:3). Moses called himself the most humble man in all the earth, but he definitely had to walk it out. He had some long journeys, did things at God's command that people did not like and had to deal with a lot of jealousy and criticism from some pretty hard people enduring long years in the desert.

In the simplest terms, humility means to be yielded to God in all aspects of life. People may see our surface commitment, but God is the only one who sees the depth of yielded commitment in our lives. God is the only one who sees the heart. He is the only one who sees in secret. He is the only one who sees the intimate details of a person's life. When Samuel, under instructions from God to anoint the next king of Israel, regarded the sons of Jesse, "so it was, when they came, that he looked at Eliab and said, 'Surely the LORD's anointed is before Him!'" (1 Samuel 16:6). Samuel was looking at natural attributes that would make someone a good king, but in the end the most unlikely candidate was chosen:

> But the LORD said to Samuel, "Do not look at his appearance or at his physical stature, because I have refused him. For the LORD does not see as man sees; for man looks at the outward appearance, but the LORD looks at the heart."
>
> 1 Samuel 16:7

David, a man after God's own heart, was God's choice. Was it that David was perfect? No. As we read further in Scripture, we can see some of his imperfections. God's decision was much more about David's heart of honesty, loyalty, love and worship of God. Do people still select impressive fleshly credentials over pure worship and relationship with God today? The Lord wants to help us see as He sees. His thoughts are far different from our own.

"Take heed that you do not do your charitable deeds before men, to be seen by them. Otherwise you have no reward from your Father in heaven" (Matthew 6:1). What we do, we are not

161

to do to be seen by men—Jesus made that clear. The Pharisees wanted to be seen as spiritual. They wanted to be the center of attention. This still happens today in different forms. People try to be spiritual instead of realizing that everything they do in life is spiritual. Washing the dishes is spiritual. How we help and treat others as we go about our day is spiritual. We are spiritual, so quit trying. We can spend all manner of time praying for others, serving or doing other religious activities to get some kind of result, but basic kindness makes a huge difference. Seek God first and help others in kindness; what we do in secret will be rewarded openly. "But when you do a charitable deed, do not let your left hand know what your right hand is doing, that your charitable deed may be in secret; and your Father who sees in secret will Himself reward you openly" (Matthew 6:3–4).

God sees the faithfulness of people's lives. He sees all the decisions they have made. He sees all that they have been through and the entirety of their personal histories. He sees what they have overcome. He sees how often they turn to Him for help. He sees whether the motivation of their hearts is to please people or please Him. Our faith is not to be complex but simple.

Are we critical, pharisaic, super-spiritual? Or do we offer hope to people? Do we make people feel better or worse? Do we lift people up or push them down? Are we controlling or do we let things go? Do we pretend to have all the answers or admit that we do not? Are we "know-it-alls" or do we let God be the judge? Is everything we do rooted in our intimacy with God or are we just big performers? Do we go around trying to prove ourselves or do we share His presence? Our lives are to reflect His image and carry His fragrance. We want Jesus to be glorified through us.

Realizing that God is our source is most important if we are to live a humble life. We want to live with Him moment by moment. By trusting in His grace, we learn not to trust in our own strength. This means that when we see something that needs fixing, we do not take it into our own hands to do it. Instead we give God the opportunity to deal with things. When we take things into our own hands, it typically ends up making things worse. The best thing we can do is put God first by spending time with Him to get wisdom in all things.

The Pillar of Wisdom

"The fear of the LORD is the beginning of wisdom; a good understanding have all those who do His commandments. His praise endures forever" (Psalm 111:10). The fear of the Lord is where wisdom begins. It is the Person of Wisdom who imparts wisdom and causes it to work in our lives. Wisdom has very much to do with the way we present ourselves, how we interact with God and others, the grace of our communication and the way we treat one another.

The way we live our lives conveys who we are. Wisdom builds a house (see Proverbs 9:1). Our lives represent a house, for we are dwelling places. We choose what we want to dwell in us. This world has a set of values to offer, a way of thinking and a way of doing things. God has His own way. Everything else is an imitation; nothing can replace the real thing.

"But the wisdom that is from above is first pure, then peaceable, gentle, willing to yield, full of mercy and good fruits, without partiality and without hypocrisy" (James 3:17). What God brings to us is the very substance of His life. When He indwells us, the virtues of heaven are imparted to us. Without His presence in our lives, the spirit of wisdom has no place of entry. The wisdom of this world is not the same as the wisdom from above that James referred to. The wisdom of the world and the wisdom of God are sourced from two completely different places and approaches.

"The fool has said in his heart, 'There is no God'" (Psalm 53:1). We see how important it is to "get it right" from the beginning. If we think that we can obtain wisdom in ourselves, we are deceived. A person might think he has made a wise choice, yet if God is not the source, or if He is not credited in the equation, then that person is foolish. If he is wise in his own eyes, he is foolish, for wisdom comes from God. The fear of the Lord is the *beginning* of wisdom. If we do not have the beginning, we have not started the race.

We can have understanding about something and make a good choice, but wisdom is not set in place by one right choice; it is the sum of a life lived in God's presence. God gives us wisdom and the ability to live it out. "If any of you lacks wisdom, let him ask of God, who gives to all liberally and without reproach, and it will be given to him" (James 1:5).

We have all made bad choices. We have all made mistakes. The question is, What did we learn and how did we overcome them? Did we acquire wisdom from God to learn, overcome and grow in His wisdom so that the next time we would yield to Him, growing in His grace? Or did we only slap on a Band-Aid that was no cure at all, not learning to lean on God? Here we can see more clearly that wisdom is the sum of our responses to the challenges of life. By turning to God as our source, our help and our trust, we grow in His wisdom.

Worldly wisdom operates out of the natural mind. The wisdom of God comes out of a yielded life to God through the Person of the Holy Spirit (see 1 Corinthians 2:4–5). All of us take tests in our lives. God will keep giving us these tests until we learn and pass them. The sooner we learn, the sooner He will graduate us to another blessing and another test. Through our dependency on the Spirit, we can overcome.

When we learn to ask the right questions, we can grow in His wisdom and grace:

- How do I deal with this situation? (Each is different.)
- What adjustments can I make that would help?
- How does this really work best?
- Is this really the only way this can be done, or am I limiting my effectiveness by my approach? Am I doing this a certain way because I am caught in a rotating pattern of thinking or was taught this is the only way to do something? Is this a sacred cow God would like to remove from my life?

God wants to build "a dwelling place of God in the Spirit" (Ephesians 2:22). He wants a house, a people who will be habitations and conduits of His presence. His wisdom will build us into that kind of house.

Peace in God's Presence

Ever feel as if you need more peace? Every one of us has a need for His peace. Where God's peace abides, there is no anxiety, just a tranquil rest in His presence. Peace is central to living our lives in faith. If we do not have it, everything else totters. His peace is so substantial that it keeps us in a place of calm, with perfectly yielded hearts before Him.

Jesus is the Prince of Peace (see Isaiah 9:6). We know that when He truly has lordship in our lives, His peace is going to be the predominant characteristic. Recall the time when Jesus was lying down, sleeping in the boat with His disciples (Mark 4:37–41). A storm beat down on them, shaking things up all around the boat, but Jesus remained unaffected because of the realm of peace upon His life. All the disciples were disturbed, anxious because of the tempest that surrounded them and even that Jesus was still asleep: "Do You not care that we are perishing?" they cried as they woke Him up. Jesus had only to rebuke the storm for peace to dominate the situation. He looks for the brand of faith in us that will not yield to the noise surrounding us but rather stands in quiet peace in the midst of the ruckus. The disciples were caught off guard by the storm. Jesus questioned them as He questions us: "Where is your faith?" He calls us to a realm of peace that transcends our natural tendencies.

We find our contentment first and foremost in God's presence. In knowing Him more than anything else, we will see our lives caught up in the flow of His greatness and love for us (see Isaiah 48:18). Through His peace we know the path that He has set before us. When we ask the Lord to rule our hearts, the very first sign of His presence is peace like a river.

Remember when you gave your heart to God? I recall the greatest love and peace flooding my soul. It happened in the midst of a faith-filled, worshiping community of believers. There I was practicing the presence of God and did not even know it. On the front row I sat with a friend who had invited me to his church, and we made a habit of worshiping the Lord. We were being saturated with the reality of His presence as the worship team sang "I Exalt Thee" and "Hosanna." The building blocks of worship were laid in my heart through this very organic, genuine devotion. This was the beginning of my walk with God, and heavenly deposits were being made in me that would last a lifetime, memories that I still can recall and relive. I was enormously blessed to have a good foundation laid in my life, with good, God-loving people. God wants us to rediscover the power that is found in community life, where His presence is at the center of it all. This is the place where good foundations are laid for years to come.

Life Application

- **BUILD** a good foundation. Embrace His righteousness, humility, grace and wisdom to lay a good foundation that cannot be shaken.

- **FIND** your identity in Christ. All the titles in the world, titles of position and accreditation, mean nothing apart from Christ. Our identity is found from being His own people.

- **RECEIVE** His grace in your life. When you appropriate His grace, you will have more grace for others. If there is anything good about us, it is only because of His grace.

- **ASK** for God's pure wisdom. If we ask for His wisdom, He will give it to us. Know the difference between the wisdom of this world and the wisdom of God.

11

Presence Communities

Behold, how good and how pleasant it is for breth-
ren to dwell together in unity! It is like the precious
oil upon the head, running down on the beard, the
beard of Aaron, running down on the edge of his
garments. It is like the dew of Hermon, descending
upon the mountains of Zion; for there the LORD
commanded the blessing—life forevermore.

Psalm 133

Finding a community centered around God's presence causes
our experience with His presence to increase exponentially.
My walk with the Lord began in a small Friday-night Bible
study. It was the best thing going on on the planet. I thought it
was better than Sunday mornings, because I had found a way
to develop friendships that would last a lifetime. This happened
through our continual commitment to one another in the simple
context of a weekly Bible study.

Commitment is essential to our lives, and it is a two-way
street. Both parties need to be committed for relationships to

go deep. Relationships are something that we just cannot do without. In them we are tested in our differences in many ways. We learn to love each other as we grow together. Is that not what Jesus told us to do, to love one another? How are we going to do that apart from community? God created us for this.

Our beginnings are a big deal. Sometimes the smallest things have a huge impact; many times the things that we think are big have little impact. A good start in your spiritual walk can determine how well the rest of your life progresses in the Lord. When I came into this small community fellowship, I had issues just like anyone else. We set a chair in the center of the room for people who needed prayer. When it was my turn to sit in that chair, God set me free from things that had weighed me down for years. That was a good jump start for my life. But even after a beginning like that, some things only surface with time. They get worked out in relational conflicts, disagreements and plain old family matters. Community works the same way that family does. Because families are often dysfunctional these days, many never get a chance to experience what a true family committed to love is like.

That is just one side of community, the relational one. But being a part of God's family holds much more for us. His presence should be the main thing we experience when we get together. It was the presence of God that kept me coming back to those Bible studies week after week. Yes, I enjoyed the people. But if God had not been in the place, it would not have worked for me. All the same, others who came did not stick. Our desire for God always weighs in to the equation. I had an earnest desire for God, a real hunger for change. God was meeting with me personally, no matter what anyone else's experience was.

As imperfect as it was, we had a common commitment to God. People were imperfectly seeking Him. Some had more issues than others. Some were more willing to deal with their issues than others. Everyone was challenged in the heart to follow the Lord. Looking back, I recognize those who had the appearance of spirituality but who never really took root. Then there were the ones least likely to succeed or stay committed who nevertheless did. All of us have to pass the test of time. We cannot be enamored with shooting stars, for God sees the end from the beginning.

One invaluable benefit to my life was the simplicity of the teaching in our group. We approached things at a very basic level. We interacted on the subjects of faith, love for God and others and the life of Jesus. Keeping Him at the center was a powerful anchor for my soul, for I always knew where to turn. Only time could weed out many of the issues in my soul. I believe this is the natural process God set in motion. He brings things to the surface in a natural progression, helping us to grow healthy rather than superficially.

Community Benefits

The benefits to being a part of a community of God's presence are myriad. We learn to love. People serve to hold us accountable for our actions. Ultimately our accountability is to the Lord, but people help keep us in check. This is why God puts us in His Body; we need one another. We grow together as a habitation of His presence (see Ephesians 2:22). We learn to respect, honor and serve one another despite some differences, coming to grips with the fact that no one is perfect, all have issues and some have more issues than others. We all need grace, love and help. The community serves as a support system and hedge of protection for our lives when it is rooted in the presence of God.

Jesus prayed that we would be one as He and the Father are one. Psalm 133 describes how, when we dwell together as one in His presence, it is like the oil of His glory being poured out upon us. In the context of community in God's presence, people need healthy relationships. Whether in groups big or small, relationships are key to our growth in Christ. God is completely into community. But community alone is not what God wants. He wants to be in the midst of our communities. It is not enough to have things that bring people together, if God's presence is not present. If He is left out of the equation, then there really is no point in coming together.

Community alone is not effective for true transformation of lives. God's presence must be the central focus. He is the glue that holds all things together. It is God who commands the blessing because we are coming together as one in His presence. We see a certain atmosphere created when we welcome the presence of God together. The oil of His anointing is poured out; a pleasant experience is created; we have love for God and one another because we are welcoming His Holy Spirit. On top of all of this, His blessing is *commanded* upon our lives. Do you want that?

Our community, our unity and where are hearts and minds come together are in the presence of God. He is the common denominator. It is not enough to have God in your head. It is not enough to have all the Scriptures memorized. All Scriptures testify of a Person, Jesus. He is the author of the book. He is also the author and finisher of our faith. Without Him we can do nothing of eternal value.

For those involved in the formalities of church, it can be easier to get caught up in the mechanics of religion, losing their first love. Jesus has to be our hearts' desire. "Church as usual" has many people caught up in organization rather than community with others. Local church can operate more like a business, country club or something to keep up and keep producing. It can be more about the numbers and less about the heart.

"Looking unto Jesus, the author and finisher of our faith, who for the joy that was set before Him endured the cross, despising the shame, and has sat down at the right hand of the throne of God" (Hebrews 12:2). At the foundation of our lives, His presence cannot be just an option for us. If His presence is not with us, we should seek Him that His presence might be with us. Then we can go out to represent Him as He is.

Community Core Values

Healthy communities are built on healthy foundations. A community centered around the presence of God should establish at its core certain values that will foster growth of the community and maturity in its people.

Refuse to Compromise

When God gathers a core group of people who have the same heart and mind in pursuing His presence—a people who refuse to settle for anything less—an amazing glory of His presence will come in the midst of His people. Sin and compromise keep us from receiving His wonderful promises. It is the "little foxes" that spoil the vine, not the big and obvious things. "Catch us the foxes, the little foxes that spoil the vines, for our vines have tender grapes" (Song of Songs 2:15).

Most people know to avoid the obvious. It is the things that people can easily hide and justify that rob them of God's life and presence. The little attitudes, gossip, criticism, people pleasing and other works of the flesh are what cause people to fall into compromise. God is looking for people who refuse to compromise, who will walk with a purity of heart. Jesus was all about the Father's pleasure. We need to have the same resolve that Jesus did in following the Father's heart, no matter what comes our way. Jesus said some very tough things. The things that He said then, He still says today.

Blessed are you when men hate you, and when they exclude you, and revile you, and cast out your name as evil, for the Son of Man's sake. Rejoice in that day and leap for joy! For indeed your reward is great in heaven, for in like manner their fathers did to the prophets.

Luke 6:22–23

Number Yourselves among the Prophets

Each of us needs a "prophetic edge" that does not compromise with the religious standards of the day. Not all are called to the office of a prophet, but we can all be prophetic because the Holy Spirit speaks to each of us as we yield to Him. When our lives are yielded to the voice of God in the Holy Spirit, we will have a prophetic element in our lives. God has promises for us, blessings to pour out on us as we follow Him.

"For He whom God has sent speaks the words of God, for God does not give the Spirit by measure" (John 3:34). Jesus was numbered with the prophets. He walked in the presence of God. He was filled with the Holy Spirit without measure. His inspiration and power came from the indwelling of the Spirit. The demonstrations of God's power came through the anointing of the Spirit. We can expect God to do amazing things as we walk with His Spirit.

Embrace the Spirit

The Holy Spirit is central to our community times as well. Without the Holy Spirit Jesus will not be glorified, for it is the Holy Spirit who glorifies Jesus. He is also the Person who creates a common bond through God's love. He pours God's love into our hearts. It is impossible to have true community without the presence of the Holy Spirit. The way we live our lives determines whether we are a Holy Spirit–friendly people.

There is a reason why His first name is "Holy"—He is holy. If we live our lives in compromise, we are grieving the Spirit. He will not form a close relationship with those who desire to follow another spirit.

Many churches are built on humanistic thinking, and the Holy Spirit is nowhere to be found. Because of this they open themselves to great deception. If the Spirit of Truth is not in a congregation, anything goes.

Seek Grace to Overcome

Most people have an understanding of grace from the standpoint of cleaning up our messes. But the grace of God enables us to overcome and live victorious lives. It is not a license to sin; John makes it clear that he who is born of God does not sin. What this means is that the person has changed from the inside out. There is no longer a desire to sin because a new Person is on the inside and a lifestyle has changed. This does not mean we are not tempted; rather our consciousness of the Holy Spirit's presence has become the dominant force in our lives. There may yet be times when we sin and need to ask forgiveness. Thankfully, "if we confess our sins, He is faithful and just to forgive us our sins and to cleanse us from all unrighteousness" (1 John 1:9).

All wrongdoing is sin (1 John 5:17), and anything that is not of faith is sin (Romans 14:23). As we grow in our understanding of what sin is, we are accountable for our actions. We are also accountable if we choose to remain ignorant and not grow in the Lord. Carnal Christians exist. These are people who have not grown up. God can trust such a person only to a degree because of that person's struggles with sin, weaknesses and immaturity. But God works with us in order to grow us up.

Some are sincerely trying to change and just do not know how. Others are not making any effort to change whatsoever.

God knows the difference and will give grace to the one who is really making an effort to change. God's grace helps us overcome and be victorious, not to sin or be lethargic. Laziness will never gain the favor of God.

Acknowledge the Gravity of Sin

A heretical teaching that has grown popular in some circles says that because your sinful nature was destroyed, you therefore cannot sin. The fruit of this teaching is a rebellious spirit and divisiveness. Those who have partaken of it have dishonored people, causing division. They are not correctable because they have nothing to correct since, they believe, they have already been made perfect. If this movement is not a cult, it is close to it (see 2 Peter 2:1–3).

This teaching has led some into other heresies such as the doctrine that there is no hell. Yet hell is a very real place, and Jesus taught of its existence, promoting the fear of God: "It is better for you to enter life lame, rather than having two feet, to be cast into hell, into the fire that shall never be quenched—where 'Their worm does not die, and the fire is not quenched'" (Mark 9:45–46). He continued, "But I will show you whom you should fear: Fear Him who, after He has killed, has power to cast into hell; yes, I say to you, fear Him!" (Luke 12:5).

Even Paul had to rebuke Peter for sin:

> Now when Peter had come to Antioch, I withstood him to his face, because he was to be blamed; for before certain men came from James, he would eat with the Gentiles; but when they came, he withdrew and separated himself, fearing those who were of the circumcision. And the rest of the Jews also played the hypocrite with him, so that even Barnabas was carried away with their hypocrisy.
>
> Galatians 2:11–13

Here was Peter, a man who was with Jesus from the inception of His earthly ministry, falling from grace and missing the mark—in other words, sinning. The point is that all of us are still able to sin. For most this is probably not an issue for their own understanding, but some need to realize that absolutely anyone can fall. We have access to grace, but it is not forced upon us. While we are on the earth, we are not perfected. If we were, then Paul would not have yearned to be with the Lord, rather than in his wretched body. "For I am hard-pressed between the two, having a desire to depart and be with Christ, which is far better. Nevertheless to remain in the flesh is more needful for you" (Philippians 1:23–24).

Cast Off Sin's Shackles

"Our old man was crucified with Him, that the body of sin might be done away with, that we should no longer be slaves of sin" (Romans 6:6). Our sinful nature was destroyed on the cross when Jesus died. When He died, we died. We are new creations in Christ. Because the sinful nature is destroyed, sin no longer has dominion over us; that does not mean, however, that we do not still have the ability to be selfish and sin. God did not take our choices away. We still have a will, with the power to choose which way we will follow. We can still blow it and sin. But sin is the exception, not the rule. We are saints, not sinners; because the sinful nature has been destroyed, we are now able to choose to live by the Spirit.

Establish Community on the Rock

Our communities must be based in the truth of God's Word. Many deceptions float around various Christian circles, but the Word of God anchors us so that we are not caught up in delusion. The Word of God is our absolute authority. If people do not believe this, they might as well go write their own Bible and start a cult.

Our thoughts need to line up with what has been clearly revealed in the Word of God, not with the whims or philosophies of the world. The Word of God is the Rock that we can stand on, the Scriptures the standard by which we live. Humanism is merely a counterfeit masquerading as good works. It is the exaltation of self, man and man's achievements. The tower of Babel exemplifies the spirit of humanism raising its ugly fist toward God, saying, "I can do this without You!" God came down, confused their languages and scattered them abroad throughout the earth.

This is why it is so important for us to embrace and demonstrate what it looks like to be completely dependent upon God in our communities—even as church families. We are actually in a dependent relationship with God; we abide in the vine so that the Lord can release the fullness of His blessing and presence in the community as a whole.

Exalt God's Presence

God wants us to have unity in the Spirit in which Jesus is exalted, the Word of God is believed and love is exemplified. There is nothing more amazing and beautiful than when believers gather together in the presence of God. When God is welcomed, it makes all the difference. Our lives are changed, transformed and liberated as His Holy Spirit dwells in our midst.

"In [the Lord] you also are being built together for a dwelling place of God in the Spirit" (Ephesians 2:22). God is building communities of His presence, people dwelling in relationship with God and others, believers living as corporate habitations of His presence. These communities will be exemplary in God's life, places where people will walk in love for one another—a magnetic draw to people in the world.

The Holy Spirit is essential for us to have the love of God in our hearts. Without God's love we cannot love one another.

Jesus made it clear that people will know that we are His disciples through the love that we have for each other. The Holy Spirit is the Person of the Godhead who makes this possible.

How important do you think it is to welcome the Holy Spirit into our gatherings? This is hugely important to the spiritual vitality of church life. There is a gigantic hole that can only be filled by the Holy Spirit being with us. What testimony do we have if God is not with us in His manifested presence? None. God's presence should be the distinguishing mark when we gather together. People who do not know God should be able to tell a difference when they come into our circle, whether they know what that difference is or not. Jesus understood that the Holy Spirit was not an option for His disciples. His first command was not to send them out to be witnesses or build a church; instead He told them to wait in Jerusalem until the Holy Spirit clothed them.

God is not as concerned with quantity as He is quality. He is looking for uncommon vessels that will carry His uncommon presence. He knows what He can do with just one that is fully committed to Him. In the same way, a community of God's presence is not about the size of a church or whether it meets in a big building or a house. Both work, but God is not looking for either; He is looking to be invited. If He is not welcome in a place, then it is nothing more than humanistic effort. God is to be at the center of our communities. The substance of His presence is what makes the difference in regard to the life of our gatherings, communities and congregations. The unsaved can tell the difference. They can see when something is a social club, political or motivated by money. God desires to see His people welcome His presence once again. There is hope for all on this side of heaven. It is time to respond to His knocking at the door and let Him in.

Life Application

- **FIND** a community of believers who love God's presence. The presence of God is vital to the life of any church community. Find a place that believes the Bible and loves the presence of the Holy Spirit.

- **BE** holy. We all have the ability to make choices. Take responsibility for your life. You are the only one who can choose the direction your life will take. Welcome the Holy Spirit to fill you as you choose to walk in His ways.

- **DISCOVER** the new life inside you. If you have given Christ your life, He makes you a new creation. Each day choose to seek the Lord, spending time with Him. Find other believers who will help you walk in the ways of God.

- **STUDY** the Bible each day. Psalm 1 promises a flourishing life to those who make the Word of God their continual meditation.

12

Visions of Glory

Awake, O north wind, and come, O south! Blow
upon my garden, that its spices may flow out. Let my
beloved come to his garden and eat its pleasant fruits.

Song of Songs 4:16

I want to share some encounters and visitations that I have
experienced in the presence of God, that you might be
encouraged to pursue the Lord. May you have more such experiences with Him in your own life.

The Song of Intimacy

God wants to breathe a new song of intimacy that will draw
hungry people into a fresh wave of His presence, even in the
driest of places. I had a dream several years ago in which a man
was singing a song in an evangelical church. He began to sing
from a hard, dry religious place in his soul, but then it blos-
somed into a song of intimacy with God as the Bridegroom.
Just as in the verse above from the Song of Songs, the sound

came like wind from the "north," heaven above, blowing on the garden of dry religion to bring forth fruit and life. As the man began to sing about the Bridegroom's embrace, pockets of people in this stagnant congregation awakened to the presence of God. The spirit of revival was released through the intimate sound on these people. It was an amazing sight, this awakening in God's glory as people began to stand in His presence. An atmosphere had been created in which all things were possible, because God was in His Church. This is a picture of how the song of our intimacy with God is needed to break through religious ritualism and usher in a fresh wind of His presence. Our intimate worship of God opens the heavens for people to encounter His glory like never before.

When the anointing is present, it has the ability to cut into places of the heart that have remained unmoved by all other efforts. When the sound of intimacy is released, the fresh waters of His presence are rediscovered, and God finds a resting place in our hearts.

One time the Lord gave me a song of intimacy through a dream. When I woke up with this song, the presence of God was tangible in the room. I immediately pulled out a recorder to capture it. The song reminded me of those produced by Maranatha! Music in the 1970s, a simple worship song with a very unique melody that captured the heart. A few days later I was leading worship at our church. The worship was good that morning, but it was a little difficult to break through into the intimate presence of God. I had prepared the song I had dreamed of as the last song. Singing it was like dropping a Holy Spirit bomb in the room. Instantly the atmosphere changed. Everyone was immediately aware of the awesome and intimate presence of God in the place. This is one example of how the song of intimacy anointed by the Spirit breaks open the atmosphere for people to experience His presence.

The intimate song of the Lord brings a fresh wind. The shock of the freshness of God's presence on cold hearts creates a greater potential for experience and impact on people. A cold air front hits a warm air front in a clash, and the results are clearly seen. This is why Jesus says in the book of Revelation that He would rather His people be hot or cold rather than lukewarm: "I know your works, that you are neither cold nor hot. I could wish you were cold or hot. So then, because you are lukewarm, and neither cold nor hot, I will vomit you out of My mouth" (Revelation 3:15–16). When people are lukewarm, they have typically grown numb to God's presence, making it harder for them to notice when God comes in the power of His Spirit. His presence is not as obvious because of the compromised state of the heart. When people want the best of both worlds, it makes them indifferent to displays of God's glory.

"And when the Chief Shepherd appears, you will receive the crown of glory that does not fade away" (1 Peter 5:4). In this Bridegroom awakening, God desires to place a crown of glory upon the heads of His people, a garland of grace so that they walk in His life, power and authority. The garland is significant, as it is a wreath composed of living things, leaves and flowers. It also represents the fresh life of His presence upon our heads, a fresh way of thinking that flows from His Spirit. Jesus brings the cure to religious stagnancy, saying, "Come dine with Me!" We are invited to taste and see that the Lord is good. When we respond, coming to taste of God's goodness, the eyes of our hearts are opened to see and know that He is good.

Entering the No-Gravity Zone

God does not give us faith for what is possible but for what is impossible. He does not want to hold us down but release us into a place without limitations, a no-gravity zone. When we grab hold of the reality that God does not limit us but rather pushes us to move outside of our comfort zones, we experience His goodness and freedom. In this place our faith thrives to believe God to do things that are far out of our own capabilities. "Jesus looked at them and said to them, 'With men this is impossible, but with God all things are possible'" (Matthew 19:26).

As overcomers we are called to live in the high places of His presence, far above all earthly entanglements—places of amazing freedom, where we realize the fulfillment of His promises to us. Jesus gives us His authority, ability and power to live lives that are exceptional before Him. There is ease, lightness and peace as we live in the reality of His glory. "For whatever is born of God overcomes the world. And this is the victory that has overcome the world—our faith" (1 John 5:4). We will always have obstacles to overcome—this is the reason why we need to live in a place of overcoming power. God has provided the means for us to overcome because of what His Son has done. We are seated in the heavenly places with Christ, far above all authority and dominion (see Ephesians 1:3, 20–21). As we embrace a life that pays the price to see His promise manifested in our lives, we will grow strong in Him.

It is God's heart to see us soar in a place of freedom where nothing holds us down. How we live, however, is determined by what we think. We can live under the limitations of a prison of lies, or we can live the unlimited life of freedom in the truth of Christ. In heaven, who we are is settled. When we allow God to take over our thinking, we will find His peace being established in our hearts. With hearts of revelation, our eyes will be opened to understand God's Word, transforming our minds to see from His perspective.

There are stories of supernatural testimony stored in heaven. These stories are just waiting to become manifested through our lives, for they have yet to be written on the earth. Through faith we can see heaven on earth manifested as His goodness changes people's lives. The cloud of witnesses is cheering us on to see these heavenly feats become reality in our lives.

God's Manifested Glory in the Earth

We are blessed to be a part of His glorious plan of the ages. Enter into the no-gravity zone by embracing a life of absolute faith, walking in the authority He has given you. Embrace a heart that overflows with thanksgiving to God for His goodness in your life. Surrender your mind and take on His nature, His ways and His thoughts. You are the person God wants to fill and flow through!

"For [the time is coming when] the earth will be filled with the knowledge of the glory of the LORD, as the waters cover the sea" (Habakkuk 2:14). We are living in a time when God wants to pour out His manifested glory throughout the earth like never before. God, the "Desire of All Nations" (Haggai 2:7), is determined to display Himself in ways we have never seen. The harvest is ready for the reaping. As His love and glory are manifested through His people, Jesus will be lifted up and men will be drawn to Him (see John 12:32). People need to encounter the living God, and the encounter God wants them to experience, He wants to give—through you!

"In whom you also are being built together for a dwelling place of God in the Spirit" (Ephesians 2:22). As we develop a lifestyle of welcoming the Holy Spirit in our lives, God will flow through us like a river. Let God use you to manifest His glory to people who do not know Him. Determine to live in His presence every day. Engage in worship. Be filled with the Spirit. Be a spout where His glory flows out!

> Therefore we also, since we are surrounded by so great a cloud of witnesses, let us lay aside every weight, and the sin which so easily ensnares us, and let us run with endurance the race that

is set before us, looking unto Jesus, the author and finisher of our faith, who for the joy that was set before Him endured the cross, despising the shame, and has sat down at the right hand of the throne of God.

Hebrews 12:1–2

Throw off all that hinders to run the race. All the things that block the flow of His presence and are not produced by His grace need to go. Determine to be all that God has called you to be. Pursue the Lord in such a way that He is a living reality in your life. An entire generation is ready to enter into this life as new creations in Christ. All they need is someone to lead them into this amazing experiential life with God.

Interceding from Heaven's View

Having seated us in the heavenly realms with Christ, God has made us intercessors with His Son. When we have an established place of intimacy with God, we then have the great responsibility and privilege of joining Jesus where He ever lives to intercede in the heavens (see Hebrews 7:25).

We are positioned to intercede from heaven's view. "And He raised us up together with Him and made us sit down together [giving us joint seating with Him] in the heavenly sphere [by virtue of our being] in Christ Jesus (the Messiah, the Anointed One)" (Ephesians 2:6 AMPC). We are seated in the highest place that exists—the heavenly realms with Jesus Christ. Jesus has welcomed us to the most privileged place to reign with Him as kings and priests. His sacrifice and blood have made this possible. God wholeheartedly desires us to grab hold of this powerful revelation of our position in Him. It is just as Jesus said, "If you abide in Me, and My words abide in you, you will ask . . ." (John 15:7). Our intimacy with God gives us weight with God, authority in our lives to pray as Jesus asked us to pray: His Kingdom come and His will be done on earth as it is in heaven.

We are part of God's plan to expand His Kingdom. As His love and authority are released through our lives, His light shines and the veil of darkness is removed from those who do not know Him. Looking down from our seated place with Christ, we realize our authority with Christ. We are not interceding from underneath the clouds but above them. God has set us above all things and comes to dwell inside of us. As we yield in intimacy and intercession, there will be an increased manifestation of the glory of heaven upon us and through us. This will result in the eyes of others being opened to the reality of God, with demonstrations and manifestations of His power.

Reflections and Exhortations

In the encounter I described in chapter 9 when I dreamed that my iPhone melted, I understood that God is going to pour out His glory in such a way that people will not be able to market it. Right now we see an element of prostitution of the things of God among His people. That will no longer work if we want to see a continued demonstration of God's power. We cannot use what God is doing to promote ourselves. God will get all the glory and will make sure of it. His power is going to melt our earthly minded approaches to things. Just as Uzzah touched the Ark of His presence foolishly and presumptuously (see 2 Samuel 6:3–7), we need to realize that God does not need our "Hamburger Helper." Just give Him the glory and move on.

God has graced us with His glory dwelling inside of us. When He performs wonders, signs and miracles without our hands or through our hands, we defer the glory to Him, making sure we are not touching His work to foster our own agenda.

187

The Church's Finest Hour!

In another dream I was shown a blue ribbon like one you would receive as a prize in a contest. On it was written, *The Church's Finest Hour!* The Lord was showing me that we are on the cusp of the greatest hour that that Church of Jesus Christ has ever known.

> Arise, shine; for your light has come! And the glory of the LORD is risen upon you. For behold, the darkness shall cover the earth, and deep darkness the people; but the LORD will arise over you, and His glory will be seen upon you. The Gentiles shall come to your light, and kings to the brightness of your rising. Lift up your eyes all around, and see: They all gather together, they come to you.
>
> Isaiah 60:1–4

A greater level of darkness will be released in the earth, but this is only an indication that our light will shine even brighter, with a greater glory of His presence! Things will become very black and white. God will make a distinction for His people who walk in the light of His presence in obedience to Him.

When we look at Isaiah 60, we hear the words *arise* and *shine*. In the original Hebrew the word for "arise" is the same word that is used for "decree." The spirit of this verse means "to rise up and decree." The word for "shine" means "to be set on fire" or ignited. The combination of these two words carries a potent meaning: "Rise up to decree the heart of God and be lit on fire!" I have taken the liberty of using my Hebrew dictionary to create my own rendition of this verse: "Arise and decree the heart of God and be set on fire, for your Illuminating Light has come, and the *kabod* of the eternal God's weighty glory is breaking out, shining forth beams of light upon you."

This is the time for our illumination, the time for our rising and shining, for we are living in the greatest hour the Church has ever seen. What may seem like a sleeping giant is about to awake and illuminate the earth with God's glory. The word for glory in this passage, *kabod*, refers to the weighty glory of God's presence.

As the Church rises to the occasion with unhindered and unbridled passion, all the things that weigh her down will be left in the dust! Because of this passionate pursuit of God, a complete surrender to His heart, the things that have hindered will be left behind, just as the wind will blow off debris when someone is running full throttle. The Church will be remantled with the weighty glory of His presence, and His glorious light will shine through us.

With Jesus at the center of our lives, all things that concern us revolve around Him in perfect harmony. Stuff that seemed like a big deal is no longer of any importance. Then all things that are of God's heart will be set before our eyes as we lay hold of the prized possession of His presence. We are living in the Church's finest hour. Arise and shine today, for greater is the glory of God inside of you than any obstacle that will come before you!

Father, I ask that You would touch Your people now in such a way that they would know the reality of Your presence in their lives. Thank You for helping them realize that they are significant in Your sight, created to live in Your presence and part of Your plan to help others experience Your love. Holy Spirit, fill them with Your love, peace and presence, that they would be used to bless others with Your grace and truth. Jesus, give them a willingness to follow Your ways, to embrace Your call and to know the sufficiency of Your grace in their lives, that they may walk in Your fullness and footsteps.

In the most powerful name of Jesus, So be it.

Life Application

- **ASK** the Lord to fill you with the intimate sound of worship, that you might grow closer to Jesus in your own devotional life.

- **BE** an overcomer. Choose to live your life as an overcomer, realizing that tough things come in your life as opportunities for victory and become your own personal testimony in the Lord.

- **JOIN** Jesus Christ as an intercessor in order for His love to fill the earth. Be a bridge that people can cross to experience the reality of life in Christ on the other side.

- **REALIZE** that you are a part of His glory covering the earth as the waters cover the seas. God wants to use you to touch people all around the globe. Think bigger and believe bigger because your God is big.